PRAISE FOR

GUIDE TO MANAGING TECHNOLOGY WITH CHILDREN AND TEENS: THE PARENTAL INTELLIGENCE WAY

"In her splendid book, *Unlocking Parental Intelligence*, Dr. Hollman showed parents how to find the meaning in their child's or teen's behavior by reflecting on the child's thoughts and feelings, which may well be different from their own thoughts and feelings about the situation. Finding the meaning underlying the behavior helps parents respond sensitively and supportively. Dr. Hollman's new book gives an excellent overview of the impact of technology in children's and teens' lives today. She then gives a concise account of Parental Intelligence methods and shows, with the aid of helpful real-life examples, how to use these methods to solve problems caused by technology. An excellent resource!"

—JANET WILDE ASTINGTON, PHD

Professor Emeritus, Institute of Child Study, Department of Human Development and Applied Psychology, University of Toronto; Editor, *Minds in the Making*

"In this volume, *The Busy Parents Guide to Managing Technology with Children and Teens: The Parental Intelligence Way*, Dr. Hollman takes on a current and rapidly growing source of difficulty in our modern world: technology. This includes the use of cell phones, tablets, computers, video games, etc. Our young people's lives have been affected in a variety of ways. Inevitably, difficulties arise. Using the Parental Intelligence method, which she again outlines here, Dr. Hollman show us how to identify the underlying problems. Then, armed with this knowledge, parents learn how to help young people manage the complicated role of 'screens' in their daily life. I found the section on 'cyberbullying' particularly useful. We are now dealing with a new kind of bullying, which has expanded exponentially with the use of social media. Using this technique, which fosters adult-child dialogue and mutual understanding, is an important way to address and resolve the problems that arise in this ever-expanding world of technology. I highly recommend this book."

—BARBARA G. DEUTSCH, MD

Certified in Psychiatry, American Board of Psychiatry and Neurology, Adult and Child Psychiatry; Certified in Psychoanalysis, American Psychoanalytic Association, Adult and Child Psychiatry

"Please read this book!

Dr. Laurie Hollman has once again given us the gift of her caring, insightful, and practical methods to help us all in our efforts to raise our children (from infancy to the late teen years) and improve all of our relationships in our personal and professional lives.

Dr. Hollman clearly explains the methods which can help all parents (and therapists) develop thoughtful, empathic channels of communication which will allow for parents and children to discover the meaning of their particular disturbance.

By following the steps of Parental Intelligence and not acting impulsively, parents can help themselves and their children find the meaning behind the immediate problems associated with the impact of technology on the lives of children and adolescents and then work together to solve the problems that become clarified in their discussions.

Through a series of easily understood explanations and the creative use of anecdotes to clearly illustrate the principles involved, Dr. Hollman takes the reader on a journey about technology today which illuminates the pathway to enhanced understanding and compassion for our dearest partners and children.

Please read this book!!! It can make a profound addition to your life."

—ERNEST KOVACS, MD, FAPA

Associate Clinical Professor of Psychiatry, Albert Einstein College of Medicine; Supervisor for Marital and Family Psychotherapy, Zucker Hillside Hospital Northwell Health

"Dr. Hollman tackles one of the most difficult aspects of parenting in *The Busy Parent's Guide to Technology*. By utilizing Parental Intelligence (*Unlocking Parental Intelligence: Finding Meaning in Your Child's Behavior*) along with insightful information and case studies focused on rapidly changing cultural norms influenced by technological advancements,

Dr. Hollman provides practical, thoughtful, and grounded guidance in navigating the often daunting and ever-changing landscape that has become one of the greatest challenges we face in raising our children and adolescents into compassionate and independent critical thinkers. A must-read for all parents and family members, professionals, or lay persons interacting with our most precious asset; the next generation!"

—LYNN SESKIN, PSYD

Clinical Psychologist; Behavioral Medicine Associates of New York; Behavioral Medicine of Pennsylvania

"Technology now plays complex roles in child development and in how parents interact with their children. In Dr. Hollman's book, she provides an insightful process through which parents can respond to and deal with this challenge in their children's development."

—JEREMY CARPENDALE, PHD

Professor of Developmental Psychology, Department of Psychology, Simon Fraser University

OTHER BOOKS BY
LAURIE HOLLMAN, PHD

Unlocking Parental Intelligence: Finding Meaning in Your Child's Behavior (Familius, 2015)

The Busy Parent's Guide to Managing Anxiety in Children and Teens: The Parental Intelligence Way (Familius, 2018)

The Busy Parent's Guide to Managing Anger in Children and Teens: The Parental Intelligence Way (Familius, 2018)

The Busy Parent's Guide to Managing Exhaustion in Children and Teens: The Parental Intelligence Way (Familius, 2020)

Are You Living with a Narcissist? How Narcissistic Men Impact Your Happiness, How to Identify Them, and How to Avoid Raising One (Familius, 2020)

The

BUSY PARENT'S
GUIDE to MANAGING
TECHNOLOGY
WITH CHILDREN AND TEENS

Published by Familius LLC, www.familius.com
1254 Commerce Way, Sanger, CA 93657

Familius books are available at special discounts for bulk purchases, whether for sales promotions or for family or corporate use. For more information, contact Familius Sales at 559-876-2170 or email orders@familius.com.

Library of Congress Control Number
2020936489

Print ISBN 9781641701938
Ebook ISBN 9781641703147

Printed in the United States of America

Edited by Kaylee Mason, Sue Franco, and Alison Strobel
Cover design by Carlos Guerrero
Book design by Ashlin Awerkamp

10 9 8 7 6 5 4 3 2 1
First Edition

The

BUSY PARENT'S GUIDE to MANAGING TECHNOLOGY

WITH CHILDREN AND TEENS

THE PARENTAL INTELLIGENCE WAY

LAURIE HOLLMAN, PhD

To Jeff, for his loving compassion and empathy as a husband and father.

ACKNOWLEDGMENTS

I am grateful to three generations of those who have inspired and helped me with this book. I must begin with my husband, Jeff, whose talented writing and editorial skills along with his empathy for children have always strengthened my resolve to put my ideas into words.

In the next generation goes my gratitude to my older son, David, who was raised with Parental Intelligence. I watch David as a father and Claire as a mother carrying out Parental Intelligence with their school-age sons. Both discussed parenting with me, clarifying my ideas. Observing their empathy as parents gives me lasting joy.

My appreciation further extends to my younger son, Rich, also raised with Parental Intelligence. Rich as a father and Shelley as a mother are wonderful examples of parents using loving Parental Intelligence with their daughter. Discussing babyhood with them also clarified my ideas with regard to how Parental Intelligence works so well even during a baby's first year.

Working with the Familius team is always gratifying. I appreciate the publisher, Christopher Robbins, for his accessibility and encouragement as I write for Familius. I am fortunate to work with Brooke Jorden, the managing editor at Familius, who introduced me to the talented editor of this book, Kaylee Mason, who meticulously read each word, gave thought to my concepts, and succeeded in her collaborative way to refine my book and bring it to fruition. Her careful attention to detail, her warm spirit, and facility with language were just what I needed.

I can't conclude without thanking the next generation in line. Thank you, Zander (age 12) and Eddie (age 9), my loving grandsons. Hearing their remarkable use of language at such young ages and watching their vibrant spirits always inspire me to keep on writing. They set the best examples of when we *want* to see kids use technology wisely. When they are playing video games, sending messages, or creatively designing their own films, it is after a day of work and play, carried out with vibrant spirit and delight for all they accomplished. It is my pleasure to also see to whom they relate with so empathically. When they confide in me their personal thoughts and wishes, I am reminded of the essence of Parental Intelligence: the close bonds it brings between parent and child, grandparent and grandchild. Thank you also little Hazel, just nine months old, who has yet to know how her spirit is videoed and photographed on her parents' cell phones, bringing joy to all who see her. Her parents, Rich and Shelley, are carefully not giving her screens to look at, waiting until she's old enough to understand them. Their thoughtful attention to her needs with loving cautions for the impact of technology on infants sets a wonderful example for other parents.

CONTENTS

INTRODUCTION

*Y*oung minds are constantly developing, as the brain matures until age twenty-five. Busy parents need to consider this as they explore the many options of online usage for their children and teens. Some medical experts claim that the brains of our children's generation are physically developing differently because of frequent interaction with technology, which impacts their communication skills. Technological usage can affect the parts of the brain that control a child and teen's personality. This can affect the way kids interact in that there might be changes in their ability to regulate emotions, remember certain events, and pay attention to different things. Parents should take all of this into consideration as they consider how to communicate with their children.

MIT professor Sherry Turkle says that technology can have a negative effect on our emotional lives. Many teens have trouble separating from their parents and becoming independent, because their parents are always just a text away. Kids can feel quite alone at times when they only communicate online—and this problem is starting very young. A recent Stanford study found that girls as young as eight were spending time multitasking digital devices and that it resulted in lowered self-confidence and social skills. Given the technology revolution, busy parents need to look at this new information and decide how to raise emotionally stable children.

Busy parents are also worried about cyberbullying, a form of aggressive harassment that is unprovoked and repeatedly directed toward another child, teen, or group of individuals. Bullying may inflict harm on the targeted youth—including physical, psychological, social, or educational harm. Busy parents need to know how to recognize and help their children if they are bullied or the bullies themselves. Conservative estimates state that at least 5 percent of those in primary and secondary schools, children ages seven to sixteen, are victimized by bullies each day, but the percentage may be higher.

Busy parents need a structured approach to solving problems their children and teens now face due to the rise in technology. The Parental Intelligence Way is a five-step approach to solving the puzzling problems of today's youth. In this book, I will explain and explore Parental Intelligence so that busy parents feel more confident in helping their children through the technological maze.

Empathic parents tend to raise empathic children, who become interested in how their parents think and feel and may become quite good at listening themselves, an aptitude experts say is lacking in this age of not-in-person communication. When parents are involved in their children's daily lives, they can better interpret what their kids are saying, helping them feel listened to and understood. Essentially, the children become more confident because their parents value their ideas and feelings. The Parental Intelligence Way emphasizes empathy in parents and their kids.

There have been major findings on the next generation of children, discovered from a $300 million National Institute of Health (NIH) federal study on kids' brains and screen use. In this study, more than 11,000 kids will be studied for more than a decade. This is what has been discovered so far:

1. The brains of nine- and ten-year-olds are experiencing a premature thinning of the cortex. The meaning of this finding is unclear but significant to follow.

2. Kids who spend more than two hours a day on screens get lower scores on thinking and language tests.

3. It is now recommended by the American Academy of Pediatrics that parents avoid digital media use, except video chatting, in children younger than eighteen to twenty-four months.

4. Babies don't transfer what they learn from iPads to the real world. This means that if you give a child an app where they play with virtual LEGO bricks—virtual blocks—and stack them, and then put real blocks in front of them, they start over. They do not learn from the virtual world how to react in the real world. According to Dr. Dimitri Christakis, they don't transfer the knowledge from two dimensions to three.

5. Dr. Christakis has also done research confirming that infants are more vulnerable to screen addiction than teens. This is because the experience of making something happen is so much more gratifying to infants.

6. It is important for parents to participate with their infants and children as they use technological devices.

Dr. Kara Bagot, an investigator for the NIH study, reports that when teens' brains are scanned as they scroll Instagram (the most popular social media app), screen time stimulates the release of the brain chemical dopamine, which has a pivotal role in cravings and desires. Dr. Bagot reports that teens use the screens impulsively and use social media compulsively in order to keep getting the good feelings, suggesting screens are potentially addictive.

Teens spend an average of four and a half hours a day on their phones, resulting in a shift in how a generation of American kids act and think.

An iPhone should be a tool that you use, not a tool that uses you!

Parents who follow Parental Intelligence become meaning-makers who are deeply interested in what goes on in their children's minds and how their children's minds work as they use technology. They will become mindful of new research findings, such as those reported above. As these findings become more complete in the decades to come, utilizing Parental Intelligence will help parents to continue discovering their children's capabilities and learning the meanings behind their kids' technological behaviors and conflicts. Problem solving is a relational process, often lost in technological online communications. As children learn to communicate, their parents can realize their underlying problems; this makes children become more open than ever to hearing what their parents have to say, because they feel understood. Thus, Parental Intelligence helps in bridging generation gaps.

As parents and children feel the reciprocity of open dialogue, so different from online communications, they slowly relax and trust their open, honest, and empathic ways of relating to each other. This is the key to problem-solving the Parental Intelligence Way. Busy parents who are able to think about their children's minds manage their parent-child relationships better and are more effective in resolving inevitable conflicts and arguments.

As we face the new generations that are immersed in technology, this collaborative approach becomes more important than ever before. Children expect to be heard, respected for their technological knowledge, and empathized with as they reciprocally empathize with their parents' state of technological knowledge. The Parental Intelligence Way fits the bill.

CHAPTER ONE

THE NET GENERATION

*I*f busy parents want to know how to get along well with their kids, they need to understand the new generation's characteristics and norms. This will enable them to use Parental Intelligence (to be described in detail later) to understand the mind-set of these children and teens who will also become the new young parents. If they understand their kids' minds and stages of development, they will be able to join their collaborative mental set and solve problems with them, cementing parent-child relationships in new ways that are effective for all the generations.

That being said, it is important to note that in this book I address both the parents of Net Gen'ers and the Net Gen'ers as parents. The parents of Net Gen'ers may still be looking for guidance—as many children in their twenties are developmentally still late adolescents—and may find new discoveries about their children in this chapter, the Net Generation. However, many Net Gen'ers are currently parents themselves and are looking for help; if this is your case, keep in mind that this chapter may be more insightful in self-reflection, while the next chapter may be more helpful in understanding your child. We are living in a technologically saturated society, and I believe that in using the information in this book (whether your children are Net Gen'ers or iGen'ers) and the Parental Intelligence Way, parents can find the success they are looking for. Now let's take a look at the latest generations.

The Net Generation is eighty million strong; in 1998, the youngest was in diapers and the eldest just turning twenty, says Don Tapscott in *Growing Up Digital*. Therefore, in 2020, for example, the youngest Net Gen'ers are in their early twenties and the oldest as old as 42—many now parents themselves. When he published the book in 1998, Tapscott was thrilled and optimistic about the growth of technology as a prize for these net Gen'ers, who were learning more and faster by taking authority of their knowledge by surfing the web. By 2009, in *Grown Up Digital*, Tapscott sees the Net Generation as interactive users. He views them as the new authorities, teaching their parents how to use the web. Tapscott dates the Net Generation 1977–1997, also called Gen Y and Millennials. He characterizes them as aggressive, interactive, media-centered global communicators, instead of passive TV watchers. He says Net children search for information, develop critical thinking, investigative skills, and are critics of which websites are the best. He also says that the family is changing (and has changed) as a result, with Net Gen'ers throughout their childhood years acting as authorities that are respected by and more engaged with adults—creating an open, consensual, effective family unit. The power dynamic between students and teachers has also shifted as they, too, reverse roles. Tapscott even states that the Net Generation's brains are wired differently from the previous generation, because they are perceiving fast-moving images faster than their parents did. As kids, Net Gen'ers were stimulated more during their first wave of brain development (birth to three years old) than previous generations, and again more during the second critical period of brain development (the teenage years).

With the child as the center, kids and parents are getting along well—even though some parents coddle their children too much or become helicopter parents, hovering even at the university. Net Gen teens and young adults travel more with their parents than Boomers did, and after college they even choose to live at home for a while before entering the work world full-time and later becoming parents themselves. Tapscott views Net Gen'ers as more open and tolerant and the least-prejudiced generation ever, as the multiracial and multicultural American population mingles and marries and views themselves as happy, confident, and positive.

From the 1990s to the Net Gen era, teen suicide rates fell, pregnancy among adolescents plummeted, and drug and alcohol use dropped. Tapscott also reports on the troubling issues that arose during this time period, such as too much time multitasking online, too much stress from heavy school workloads and the college application process. All in all, there are nine differentiating characteristics of the Net Generation norms:

1. They want freedom of choice and expression.
2. They customize and personalize their lives.
3. They are the new scrutinizers of products, promotional efforts, and corporate practices.
4. They seek corporate integrity and openness.

5. They want entertainment and play in their work, education, and social life.
6. They are the collaboration and relationship generation.
7. They have a need for speed with a global database.
8. They are transforming the workforce, bringing increased collaboration, mutual influencing, and co-innovating products and services with producers.
9. They have entered formal political life, launching Barack Obama as the Democratic president and taking an active role in politics and government.

Tapscott emphasizes that this generation likes to share information. They want to connect with friends and family while they use technology—from texting and calling to social networks. He points out that with popular social networking, the internet is a place to share and connect, like a kind of cyber community center. He highlights that the internet has been transformed from a place to find information to a place where you share information and collaborate, creating new ways to solve pressing problems. He also views this generation as one that is creating content with a new paradigm of communication that will have a revolutionary impact on music and movies, political life, business, and education.

However, he cautions that these young people may not be sufficiently aware that when they share intimate details about themselves it may come back to haunt them later. They are so enthusiastic that they might not realize how much their over-sharing will potentially impact their privacy. While a popular way for Net Gen'ers under the age of thirty-five to communicate is by regularly visiting blogs (one of the most popular ways to create and share content), they may not be terribly conscious that the information they create and share is in the public domain. Privacy is a serious issue they may need to contend with in their future lives.

Also significant is that Net Gen'ers get anxious when in a hurry, and they feel a sense of deprivation if separated from their phones for more than twenty-four hours. Some don't turn off their phones and even sleep with them under their pillows.

Furthermore, through vast interactive networks, the Net Gen'ers change and add things online with comments on their blogs, corrections on Wikipedia listings, movie reviews, or YouTube videos posts. With the advent of Facebook, they began to create online communities for their friends, as well as shut people out that they didn't know or want to have in their circle. It's a community independent of time and space where they can contribute whenever and wherever they want. The social networks are virtual spaces where teens are free to shape their own identities and manage networks. Their online comments from friends provide a channel for feedback and affection—although many of these relationships are shallow, and the process plays a role in how teens learn social rules and cope with status, respect, gossip, and trust. As a result of social media's rising power, there has been a power shift from authorities to ordinary individuals. Individuals can now participate in new ways, rivaling TV by writing on Wikipedia and selling goods in e-markets like Craigslist. Essentially, as knowledge expands, power becomes more widely distributed as well.

Again, the privacy issue is paramount. The new marketing world has a new way to look into the Net Gen'er's private life, as social media profiles include names, profile pictures, genders, birthdays, and locations. Application makers see political views; activities and interests; and music, movie, book, and TV preferences. Personal details give marketers a window into the Net Gen'er world. Are Net Gen'ers setting themselves up for their basic right to be left alone? Are Net Gen'ers giving access to inappropriate postings that may one day do irreparable damage to their job and career prospects? It raises the question of who's responsible. Are social networks and other companies responsible to help educate their users and customers on this issue? After all, when users make online purchases, the information is recorded and entered into giant databases. Tapscott doesn't believe that the Net Gen'ers fully understand the long-term consequences of sharing intimate information about themselves with the world.

Tapscott goes on to report the eight norms of the Net Generation that readers need to hold in mind for when I later discuss the Parental Intelligence Model:

1. Freedom

Net Gen'ers prefer flexible hours and compensation based on performance and market value, as opposed to face time in an office. They are focused on career development and may change jobs frequently in order to meet their own needs as well as contribute significantly based on their contemporary skill set. They don't want to be stifled in a cubicle or office or to be restricted to a set desk site, which feels like being micromanaged. They want to learn and contribute.

2. Customization

Net Gen'ers are used to getting something and customizing it to make it work for them. They may sound spoiled, but perhaps we should take a second look at the fact that they've grown up getting what they want, when and where they want it, as they use their creativity to make things fit their personal needs and desires. What sounds narcissistic and self-centered is also a guide to entrepreneurial skills and overcoming challenges and obstacles creatively.

3. Scrutiny

They want to be trusted to get a job done. If that means latitude as well as an acceptance of guidance and it works, why not try it?

4. Integrity

They trust but verify the information they discover, seeking honesty, consideration, and transparency and abiding by commitments. That's not selfish; it's economical and efficient.

According to Tapscott (2009), "As parents, the early evidence suggests, they want to run their families based on such values. This is such a hopeful finding—the biggest generation ever is demanding that companies and other institutions behave with integrity. What a powerful force for a better world" (88).

5. Collaboration

Net Gen'ers naturally collaborate because they are a relationship generation, according to Tapscott. At work, they want to feel their opinions count and are respected. At the same time, while acknowledging their lack of experience, they feel they have significant insights—especially about technology and the internet. Thus, they want to have opportunities to influence decisions and to change work processes to make them more efficient. They respond to a model of education that is customized and collaborative, meaning student-focused and reciprocal.

6. Entertainment

Net Gen'ers anticipate that work should be fulfilling and fun. They do become bored easily, so need to have time for fun while being productive.

7. Speed

Having grown up digital, they expect speed, meaning they are used to instant responses and rapid feedback. This does include a touch of narcissism, but their loyalty may weaken if requests for regular feedback are not acknowledged in a short amount of time or if they feel emotionally less satisfied.

8. Innovation

Marketers are learning swiftly that Net Gen'ers want the latest and greatest products available. This again strikes of their narcissism, especially in that their fellow Net Gen'ers become envious if they do get the best of the best—as it contributes to social status and a positive self-image.

Some of these norms may seem wide-ranging, such as valuing choice, skepticism, and scrutiny while valuing being honest, considerate, transparent, and committed; thriving on speed; and loving innovation. The Net Gen mind is flexible, adaptable, and highly developed in spatial skills, hand-eye coordination, quick reaction times, and peripheral vision—all skills that are useful for architects, engineers, and surgeons. With this is mind, they can meet not only their work needs, but their family needs. Net Gen'ers are accustomed to gaming, which means high levels of trial and error and learning from failures. For those who fear their children are losing social skills due to a lack of in-person social interaction, know that this is open for debate. Some believe these kids are growing up hanging out when playing games or using the web socially, while others believe web games are distant relations without social depth.

Another area of debate is whether screen time discourages critical thinking skills. Searching for information on the web by clicking for a key word is different than reading and synthesizing different resources. But this is not to say it makes for less learning—screen searching can teach the ability to scan, navigate, and analyze pertinent information and to synthesize and remember the goals of your search. It's been suggested that the Net Gen brain is able to execute perceptual tasks rapidly and maintain more items in working memory than the brains of previous generations. The ability to be expert scanners who learn to collaborate with other people and machines is a new skill set involving multitasking and "quick switching," or juggling many sources of information in real time while tackling complicated problems. This all suggests a need for changes in educating; education should be more relevant to the skills Net Gen'ers have. For example, where learning is interactive, not rote memorization, and where kids collaborate among themselves and others outside their schools. With the new web, kids not only hunt for information but contribute to it.

Net Gen'ers know how to use the latest collaborative tools. They want to feel challenged and valued in the workplace as well as in their families, as we shall see when we delve into the Parental Intelligence Way. In fact, one out of every two Net Generation workers values family time more than work, compared with

41 percent of the boomers. Net Gen'ers expect to mix work with personal lives and be judged on their performance, not face time at work. They want their employers to manage them as individuals, not as a big group. This is a new company culture, where collaboration is how Net Gen'ers get things done. Because of their digital upbringing, they seek signs of respect and trust as they "relax into productivity, not stress into it" (Tapscott, 2009, 165).

Interestingly the mind-set of "discover and collaborate" began with online, interactive video game playing and resulted in professionals who are more loyal, flexible, persistent problem solvers and who emphasize cooperation more than individual competition. This reflects the reciprocal nature of the Net Generation, who believes in initiating, engaging, collaborating, and evolving. Money is not at the top of their list of priorities, as they want to learn, meet interesting people, and do interesting work—all while having fun. In new organizations, each employee is treated like an individual contributor, and there is a relationship and commitment from employee and employer. This taps into the needs of the individual worker who engages and collaborates, who can build a career based on new power relationships where a young person and older person become authorities in different domains. When older employees dismiss younger workers, the latter find new venues to work, because they want their expertise to be respected and valued. With the open and honest communication that mutual respect requires, the performance of organizations democratizes and accelerates.

What about the family? Tapscott reports that the Net Gen'ers are a family-oriented generation, moving home after college because they view their families as democracies where they have a say. Tapscott says:

> I think it's more important than ever for parents to talk with their kids about real human values and other important topics—at the family dinner table and elsewhere. And the good news is that the Net Generation is well positioned to take on this topic as they begin to launch families of their own. Our research suggests that this family-oriented generation will design open families that will be well suited to handling the challenges that their kids will face when they explore the world online. (2009, 221)

Tapscott's point is that children's physical freedoms were restricted, due to parents' fears about safety, and this led to teens wanting to be independent as soon as they completed high school. However, there was a shift toward a new freedom—found on the Net. Kids were the experts, not the authority figures in the house. Rebellion wasn't needed. When kids teach their parents, Tapscott calls it the "Generation Lap," which changes the power dynamic in the family. The parents of Net Gen'ers described themselves as parents who expected kids to follow rules and bear social responsibilities but were willing to discuss them openly. Parents still held the line on what was right and wrong, safe and unsafe, but kids were talked to and listened to. Net Gen'ers trust their parents and discuss serious issues with them more than their friends. We will see how this is reflected in the Parental Intelligence Way.

Other issues confront families of Net Gen'ers, such as cyberbullying. The cyberbully gets an audience of bystanders by recruiting hundreds of friends on Facebook and millions of bystanders on YouTube, posting videos of attacks. Parents are terrified of online bullying, as they want to protect their children from internet abuse. Because it can reach kids at home, it attacks them where they feel most safe. The ultimate bulwark against online bullying must exist at home in the conversations between parents and their kids. The new democratic family supports this kind of intervention. Family dialogue with busy cyber-smart parents is the best defense against the problem of bullying as well as porn and the online sexual predator.

Whether you see all of these Net Generation characteristics in yourself or in your children, you can learn from these statistics and information. Technology does not have to make the family dynamic worse, but simply requires a new set of skills and new topics of conversation. As Net Gen'ers are and will become parents, they are already experts about online bullying and democratized families, helping their kids dialogue about these threats.

I suspect that Tapscott would readily endorse the Parental Intelligence Way that will be discussed in coming chapters:

> The Net Gen'ers affinity for both the family and technology will, I believe, finally bring to life the open family. . . . Net Gen parents will collaborate with their children in creating an interactive, open family that lives according to a different model of authority—one that is topical, situational, and fluid. Net Gen'ers are quick to recognize that the best way to achieve power and control is *through* people, not *over* people. (2009, 240)

CHAPTER TWO

THE iGENERATION AND MENTAL HEALTH

Next, let's take a look at the generation that follows the Net. Net Gen'ers may find more parental insight here, as the information and statistics apply to current children and teens.

In 2014 Jean Twenge, a psychology professor at San Diego University, bemoans the fact that there is now a Me-Generation, also called the Millennials. This generation is self-absorbed and narcissistic—more tolerant than ever before but lacking in empathy and over-focused on individualism. She dates this generation as being born from 1980 to 1994. Her view is diametrically opposed to Tapscott's optimism. By 2017 Twenge is crying out about the relationship between technology and rising rates of depression among those in the iGeneration, which she dates from birth years 1995 to 2012. This iGeneration includes 74 million Americans, about 24 percent of the population. The generational changes are swift, and children are staying younger longer, pining for less responsibility and more time spent with their parents at later adolescent ages than ever before. This tendency interrupts the growth of their autonomy. The newest wave of generations is described by Twenge in her book *iGen*. Twenge highlights how individualism is still rampant, but—now that screen time and texting are at a high point—personal interaction has lowered and depression is at a high point, as well. While narcissism has lessened since the Me-Generation, mental health is in jeopardy. These trends are significant and worrisome for the busy parents of our young people. Twenge (2017) reports that as teens spend less time with their friends in person and more time on their phones, their life satisfaction drops with astonishing speed. While the iGeneration's focus is still extrinsic—focusing on money, fame, and image—unlike the Millennials, iGen'ers do not score particularly high in narcissism, which peaked around 2008 and has been on a decline ever since. iGen'ers are not as overconfident, entitled, or grandiose as Millennials were at the same age. However, the grandeur of narcissism and inflated self-esteem and entitlement during the Me-Generation is now slipping into low self-confidence, loneliness, increased suicidal risk, and depression. This new era presages high mental health risks for our teens and young adults, with significant declines in in-person social interaction. How to love when your life is spent online is the subject of this new era; as Twenge writes, "the paradox of iGen: an optimism and self-confidence online that covers a deep vulnerability, even depression, in real life" (2017, 102).

Busy parents need to contend with these threats to the mental health of their children and teens. Twenge poses the question, "Why might smartphones cause depression?" (2017, 105). She cites the following causes for mental health risks during this generation:

1. Not getting quick replies to text or social media messages causes anxiety, a common precursor to depression.

2. Social media rumors or incidents give rise to depressive thinking.

3. Parents feel helpless not knowing what their kids are doing on social media.

The rates for suicide are more pronounced in girls. Between 2009 and 2015 the number of high school girls who had seriously considered suicide in the past year increased 34 percent, and the number who attempted suicide increased 43 percent. The number of college students who seriously considered suicide jumped 60 percent between 2011 and 2016 (Twenge, 2017, 110).

This growth in suicide started around the same time that smartphones became common, suggesting very suspicious timing.

Little change in doing homework occurred from 2012 to 2016. The more time children and teens spent on homework, the less likely homework was to be a source of depression (111), concluding that pressure from studying was not the cause of the rise in anxiety and depression.

While TV watching is linked to depression, teens watch less than they used to, eliminating that as a cause.

Plausibly, more screen time has led directly to more unhappiness and depression: more screen time has led to less in-person social interaction, which then leads to unhappiness and depression; and more screen time has led to less print media usage, leading to unhappiness and depression (112).

So, as busy parents we must look at screen time as evidence for the shift in mental health issues. According to Twenge (2017), experiments that randomly assign people to experience more or less screen time and that tracked behavior over time both found that more screen time caused more anxiety, depression, and loneliness, and less emotional connection. Furthermore, it is reported that iGen'ers are unprepared for adolescence and early adulthood. This is due to their lack of independence, because they are less likely to work, manage their own money, and drive in high school. Perhaps they are not developing the resilience that comes from doing things autonomously on their own (i.e., the effects of helicopter parenting).

Too many iGen'ers are so addicted to social media that they find it difficult to put down their phones and go to sleep. Smartphone usage seems to have decreased teens' sleep times to less than seven hours a night—where they should be getting nine hours a night. (See *The Busy Parent's Guide to Managing Exhaustion in Children and Teens: The Parental Intelligence Way*, Hollman, 2020). An extensive metadata analysis of studies on electronic devices used among children revealed that kids who used a media device before bed were more likely to sleep less than they should, more likely to sleep poorly, and more than twice as likely to be sleepy during the day. The allure of the blue light of the smartphone glowing in the dark is often too difficult to resist. In sum, new media usage is both the most strongly related to sleep deprivation and the only activity that increased significantly between 2012 and 2015, when rates of mental health disorders were rising. Sleep deprivation affects mood so that those who don't sleep enough are prone to depression and anxiety, and furthermore, teens who sleep less than seven hours a night are also 68 percent more likely to have at least one risk factor for suicide (Twenge, 2017, 116). And unfortunately, depression is still stigmatized and undertreated, while genetics and environment are interacting as we see. Ultimately, sleep deprivation, the decline of in-person social interaction, and the rise of smartphones all come together to heighten mental health issues.

What are the attitudes and values of iGen'ers and how do they contribute to mental health? According to Twenge (2017), compared to the previous Millennials, more iGen college students indicate it's important to help others in difficulty, contribute to society, and hold jobs that help others. However, they aren't making these dreams a reality. Fewer iGen'ers express empathy for those unlike themselves, and while they say helping others is important, they don't think that help needs to come from them. Thus, there is a disconnect between statements and actions, as they are less inclined to be skilled at actually getting involved.

This may or may not be changing, as we see the 2017 Women's March protest Donald Trump's policies as the beginning of a new movement. Are iGen'ers taking steps toward more action than just talk? It's hard to say, as it also seems that high internet usage is linked to individualistic attitudes rather than community involvement. The generation's attitudes even show up in practical matters—like shopping. In contrast to the Millennials before them, who felt that owning something would impress their friends, the iGen'ers are more focused on the practical product for the individual, themes of safety and security, and favoring logic over emotions. However, this attitude comes with a more realistic view of careers and a greater work ethic; iGen'ers understand they need to work hard in today's economy, because their future depends on it.

Where does busy parenting fit in with the iGen'ers? Here are the following suggestions for parenting the iGen'ers:

1. Put off giving kids a smartphone for as long as possible. By the time their kids are in middle school, parents usually want to be connected to know their kids' whereabouts and safety. However, the phones are generally banned from being used in school itself.

2. Links between cell phone usage and depression are highest in younger teens. With that in mind, parents should keep an open dialogue about the use of phones. Older teens, who are more certain of their identities, are less likely to be as emotionally affected by social media.

3. Given the emphasis on sexuality found online, it's best to spare our teens that pressure for as long as possible.

In fact, many CEOs strictly regulate their own kids' tech usage. Apple CEO Steve Jobs, for example, was a busy parent who limited technology in his home; other tech experts also limit their kids' screen time. So even busy parents who love technology and make a living off of it are cautious about their kids using too much.

Electronic communication is linked to poor mental health, whereas interacting in person is linked to good mental health. The obvious conclusion is that these two types of interaction are not the same. It might explain why—especially for girls, who are the primary consumers of social media and also the primary sufferers of mental health issues—teens need to be protected by their parents. It is suggested that busy parents can limit their teens' screen usage to an hour a day; these short doses allow them to not be left out and also protected from internet addiction. Since we know that depression and anxiety have risen at unprecedented rates and that twice as many young teens commit suicide now than in past generations, it seems clear that screen time needs to be regulated. Tech detachment is today's reality. "Life is better offline, and even iGen'ers know it" (Twenge, 2017, 294).

Other suggestions for busy parents include the following:

- Before you give your teen their phone, install an app that limits the amount of time spent on it.
- Lock their phone after a certain amount of time—or even turn it off.
- Install the parental controls before you give your teen the phone. That is, before she becomes addicted to social media.
- No one, including adults, should sleep within ten feet of his phone.
- Buy an inexpensive alarm clock rather than using your phone to awaken you.
- Encourage platforms that allow for brief and individual posts over those that encourage near-permanent and group posts—such as Snapchat, with stories that last only twenty-four hours.

- Teens and adults should put their phones away when with other people in person. This can be taught as phone etiquette if parents model it.
- Contrary to popular opinion, the human being cannot multitask but focuses attention on only one cognitive task at a time. So, putting down the smartphone is crucial for study and work.
- Use the phone for a break from work and study after about forty-five minutes, and then put it away.
- Parents need to prevent children and teens from seeing pornography by discussing it in open, honest dialogue. Let your teens know that pornography does not portray normal adult sexuality.
- Finally, online time does not protect against loneliness and depression, while in-person time does. Openly and honestly discuss this with your kids so that they know what they are up against.

Overall, the ideal is that the phone is used in moderation by both busy parents and their kids. Parents should help their kids put it down and be present in the moment as much as possible in order to safeguard mental health.

CHAPTER THREE

THE PHYSICAL EFFECTS OF TECHNOLOGY

*A*dvances in technology allow children and teens to have internet access through their computers, cell phones, TV, iPods, MP3s, DVD players, and video games; and they are all vying for your kids' attention. Busy parents, teachers, and health workers are questioning the physical effects that technology has on our children's lives. I will address several effects separately: obesity, eye health, effects on the brain, physical wear and tear, ear health, and emotional health.

OBESITY

According to a 2012 review in *Obesity*, a great deal of screen time may increase the obesity risk in children and teens, as "an increase in exposure to technology goes hand in hand with a decrease in physical activity . . . , burning off calories—and energy. . . . Combined with an increase in snacking, this can lead to significant weight gain," according to studies done by Livestrong (Boyers, 2018).

It's not only that increased technology usage contributes to more sedentary behavior, but also what kids are exposed to when they watch TV. According to a report in the *Journal of the American Dietetic Association* in 2008, nine out of ten food ads shown during Saturday morning children's programming are for low-nutrient foods higher in fat, sodium, and added sugars. This food marketing influences kids' preferences and, therefore, their health. This is partly because kids have a hard time distinguishing between regular programming and advertisements.

Increased time in front of screens also leads to increased snacking with mindless eating. A study published in the *Journal of the American College of Cardiology* in 2014 that monitored the habits of 1,003 sixth graders found that those who spent more time in front of the computer, the TV, or video games snacked more often and ate fewer healthy snacks than those children who used technology less often. Another study published in the *Journal of the American Medical Association* in 2014 reported that more stimulating shows lead to a dramatic increase in snacking. Furthermore, TV in a bedroom increases screen time use and weight status. A lack of sleep causes an increase in ghrelin, the hormone that signals you're hungry, and a decrease in leptin, the hormone that signals you are full. On average, a sleep-deprived person consumes 300 extra calories per day and snacks more frequently than someone who is well-rested; this decreased amount of sleep is often associated with late-night viewing.

The American Academy of Pediatrics recommends that children and teens spend a maximum of one to two hours in front of a screen each day. It's suggested that parents should encourage their kids to get off the couch by playing with them—doing an activity they both enjoy—and working up a sweat together. Let your kid pick the plan and then block off time from other distractions—like your cell phone, which is put away (Boyers, 2018)!

TWO WAYS TECHNOLOGY AFFECTS YOUR EYES

There isn't research showing that constant technology usage causes permanent vision damage, but staring at bright screens for hours on end can lead to smaller-scale problems, said Dr. Richard Shugarman, a professor of ophthalmology at the Bascom Palmer Eye Institute at the University of Miami. Too much technology can lead to ocular discomfort, such as the following:

Tension Headaches

Extremely high contrast from lit screens causes headaches. Reading dark print on an extremely bright background can lead to spasms of the muscles at the temples, causing stress headaches. This is why e-readers—like the Amazon Kindle or the Barnes & Noble Nook, made for long reads—have black text on gray background. Reading e-books made for e-readers on cell phones, where the contrast is not made for long reads, can alternatively cause headaches. So, if you are developing headaches from reading off of a screen, it's important to decrease the contrast on your phone screen.

Dry Eye

Amanda Chan (2011) reports that when looking at something from a distance, eyes automatically blink. However, blink rate slows down when you look at things closer to your face, meaning tears evaporate more quickly when you are looking at things closer to you. So for anyone already prone to dry eyes, including contact lens wearers whose lenses sit on top of the tear film, staring closely at a screen for long periods can exacerbate dryness and cause itching, strong blinking, and grit collection in one's eyes, Shugarman reports (summarized in Chan, 2011).

EFFECTS ON THE BRAIN

There are multiple ways that technology is negatively affecting Millennials' and iGen'ers' brains, as they are the most digitally connected generations in history. At least one study concluded that the average Millennial spends up to eighteen hours per day using digital media, sometimes simultaneously. According to the scientists at the National Institute of Mental Health, many of these young minds are still developing, as the brain continues to mature until age twenty-five.

Some medical experts claim that the brains of this generation are physically developing differently because of their frequent interaction with technology, which impacts their communication skills. Technology use can affect the parts of the brain controlling the core of a person's personality, from how a person works in a team to hand gestures and expressions. Kirk Erickson, PhD and principal investigator of the Brain Aging & Cognitive Health Lab at the University of Pittsburgh, says we have not yet linked technology use and personality changes. However, he points out that texting and surfing the web use different parts of the brain than reading or speaking do. And some neuroscientists have targeted which parts of the developing brain are affected by technology usage. Researchers at the Chinese Academy of Sciences in Beijing say there have been changes in the ways the prefrontal cortex, cerebellum, and parietal lobe mature.

The prefrontal cortex, residing in the frontal lobe, controls personality, cognition, and social behavior. The cerebellum coordinates and regulates muscular activity, including those linked to language. The parietal lobe deals with interpreting language and words.

Thus, excessive use of technology, according to leading scientific publications, atrophies the frontal lobe. This breaks down ties between differing parts of the brain, resulting in the shrinking of the outermost part of the brain and making it more difficult to process information.

Erickson told *PublicSource* that these brain changes can affect the way people interact in that there might be changes in an ability to regulate emotions, remember certain events, and pay attention to different things. If this is the case, then technology use can "certainly affect how you communicate with people" (Zachos, 2015).

PHYSICAL WEAR AND TEAR

Millennials (and later generations) exemplify the long-term effects of heavy technology usage. Health problems such as neck and back pain, nearsightedness, and difficulty with offline relationships are common in this generation.

"Tech neck" is one of the most noticeable effects of cell phone use; other effects include the rewiring of certain brain structures—causing brain matter to shrink—an injured ability to regulate emotions, and internet addiction.

Health professionals blame the rise in back problems among the young on the amount of time sitting—often in front of a screen and not exercising. This sedentary lifestyle can lead to other physical problems as well, such as weight gain.

Part of the problem is that over time moods can become dependent on technology. Playing games on smartphones can give children and teens a rush by stimulating the pleasure centers of the brain. But it is reported that it can easily go the other way and lead to excessive aggression or a loss of interest in offline life.

HOW TECHNOLOGY IMPACTS EAR HEALTH

Dr. Jennifer Smullen, who works at Mass. Eye and Ear, says buds don't cause problems directly; however, "they could lead to hearing loss overtime because of the way people use them." Ear buds don't "'block out background sound so people tend to turn the volume up louder.' Over time, that can cause hearing loss or tinnitus, which is an annoying ringing in the ear. Dr. Smullen recommends over-the-ear headphones which do a better job of blocking out that background noise" (Ebben, 2012).

EMOTIONAL HEALTH

MIT professor Sherry Turkle says technology can have a negative effect on our emotional lives. Many teens have trouble separating from their parents and becoming independent, because their parents are just a text away. Kids never feel quite alone, and this problem starts very young. A recent Stanford University study found girls as young as eight spending time multitasking digital devices, which resulted in lower self-confidence and social skills. Multitasking doesn't really work, because while you feel like the master of the universe, your performance goes down—which is bad for your emotional well-being. Research even shows that the longer you sit, the greater the likelihood is that you'll die at a younger age! Turkle recommends going through your email on your smartphone while you take a walk.

As a busy parent, it is important to have this information about the risks surrounding technology. With knowledge and information, you can have educational and productive conversations with your children about how to best use technology in your home.

CHAPTER FOUR

CYBERBULLYING

*A*nother aspect of technology that has not been explained is cyberbullying. First, let's look at what bullying is. Busy parents are worried about bullying, questioning exactly how bullying is defined and how to react if their child is bullied—or being the bully. Bullying is a form of aggressive harassment that is unprovoked and repeatedly directed toward another individual or group of individuals. There is always a power differential. Additionally, bullying may inflict harm on the targeted child or youth—including physical, psychological, social, or educational harm. These are several characteristics of bullying:

1. The behavior is intentional.
2. It can be written, electronic, verbal, physical, or visual communication with the malicious and willful intent to coerce, abuse, torment, or intimidate.
3. The maliciousness is some form of violence.
4. Overt aggression includes name-calling, pushing, or hitting.
5. Relational aggression includes gossip, rumor spreading, social sabotage, exclusion, and any other behaviors harmful to interpersonal relationships.
6. By definition, a bullying behavior is repetitive, creating a dynamic where the victim worries about what the bully will do next.
7. The bully has perceived or actual power over a victim, which can include technological proficiency.

Conservative estimates state that at least 5 percent of those in primary and secondary schools, children ages seven to sixteen, are victimized by bullies each day—but the percentage may be much higher. In 2011, 27.8 percent (over 6.8 million) youth reported being bullied at school in the United States. Essentially, the proportion of teens in the US who have experienced bullying at school has remained basically unchanged over the last decade or so (Hinduja and Patchin, *Bullying Beyond the Schoolyard*, 2015, 9).

Cyberbullying is defined by Hinduja and Patchin as "willful and repeated harm inflicted through the use of computers, cell phones, and other electronic devices" (11). The essential elements are:

1. Willful: The behavior must be deliberate, not accidental.
2. Repeated: Bullying reflects a pattern of behavior, not just one isolated incident.
3. Harm: The target must perceive that harm was inflicted.
4. The use of computers, cell phones, and other electronic devices "differentiates cyberbullying from traditional bullying" (11).

The key elements are malicious intent, violence, and repetition, where cyberbullies seek pleasure or perceived social benefits by mistreating others. Through electronic means, cyberbullies often convey direct threats of physical violence carried out with some measure of maliciousness—even if it's subtle. Generally, the bullies are adolescent, and the targets cannot defend themselves.

At the same time, it is important to point out that *most* teens are not misusing the wide range of technology available now or mistreating others online. There are a huge number of social networking platforms that are uncontrolled, unregulated, unconstrained public spaces where teens can socialize and assimilate cultural knowledge in a positive way. Teens flock to these platforms, because they seem to be relatively free from direct adult supervision and control. Teens desiring autonomy and relative independence from their parents are seeking this venue naturally and have been for ages. The technological landscape is filled with the potential of bringing people together to create new personal and professional friends and relationships. This can be a great resource for both youth and their parents. However, it is safer to let others know where you are by texting individually—rather than using geotagging on phones, cameras, and laptops that have GPS coordinates or other location-based information embedded in their metadata. It is wise to disable all location sharing on Facebook, Twitter, Instagram, and other social media activity—on both your own and your child's phone.

THE NATURE OF CYBERBULLYING THAT MAKES IT MORE ATTRACTIVE THAN OTHER FORMS OF BULLYING

Simply put, cyberbullying is attractive because of its ease of use and the following key elements cited by Hinduja and Patchin (2015, 46–65):

1. Anonymity and pseudonymity

Cyberbulling has the perceived benefits of anonymity and pseudonymity—aggressors think they cannot be identified or can hide their true identity. However, thanks to IP addresses, legal authority, and financial backing, most individuals are not indeed anonymous and can be tracked.

2. Disinhibition

Like alcohol or wearing a mask at a party, cyberbullying is disinhibiting; the aggressor isn't visible and lets down his inhibitions without ready guilt and remorse.

3. Deindividuation

People lose their self-consciousness when engaging in cyberbullying, because they are influenced by the online setting rather than the reality of social norms or potential consequences. Bullies are deindividuated when their awareness of themselves and their abilities to self-regulate what they do are diminished. In cyberbullying, there is a feeling of being hidden in a group; bullies feel at liberty to act in a more immature or irresponsible and deviant manner.

4. Lack of supervision

There are no state or local laws that make sure service providers police information. However, it would be ethically and morally responsible to investigate reports of misbehavior, such as cyberbullying.

5. Virality

Harmful information can be sent to large numbers of people in a short amount of time, increasing the target's victimization.

6. Limitless victimization risk

For many users, there is no differentiation between real life and cyberspace life, making an endless arena for victimization due to cyberbullying. Cyberstalking is also a way to induce fear, threaten, and harass through technology. It is a crime in many states.

BUSY PARENTS RESPONDING TO CYBERBULLYING

The question of how to discipline the irresponsible use of social media is a large issue without clear answers. What is the busy parent to do? Preventing your child from using social media is not the answer, in fact that victimizes them further by making them outliers of the social media that their culture demands. One thing parents can do is elicit help from schools if they are made aware of a cyberbullying incident in the educational arena. There are liability concerns when technology is provided at a school or brought to a school and used to cause harm. Harassment and discrimination in general violate the Civil Rights Act of 1964 and other state and federal legislation. Thus, school personnel who fail to respond to incidents brought to their attention can be held legally responsible.

Parents and educators can then work together, addressing the bullying behavior. This leaves room for justice, as effective intervention might preclude expensive and complex litigation and claims of overstepping disciplinary bounds. It can all quickly become an invitation for lawsuits based on the first and fourth amendment rights of students. Considering these guidelines, educators can defer to parental authority when possible so that the parents of the offending student are willing to work at resolving the situation informally—creating a peaceful solution among school staff, students, and parents. At the same time, school district policies should clearly spell out the range of penalties based on the severity of bullying incidents; penalties should be proportionate to the weight of the offense and convey the extent of its gravity and severity. If the penalties are effective, the offender should know that his behavior is inappropriate and will not be tolerated—and that subsequent refusal to follow the rules will result in future disciplinary action. School policies should not let even minor forms of harassment be ignored. In fact, every cyberbullying incident should be investigated and documented. Bullying behaviors intensify when nothing is done to stop them; possibly, cyberbullying is attractive to students because it is perceived to be overlooked by adults.

Youthful victims may be wary of contacting their parents, fearing that their parents will overreact when busy and be dismissive about the extent of the impact. As parents it's important to lay the groundwork for your children and teens to feel comfortable approaching you to discuss their issues—even though you are busy. Adolescents who are cyberbullied should not suffer through the terrain alone, but they should feel that their parents are supportive and available. Swift and appropriate responses from parents will build the parent-child relationship, as we will soon discuss. Additionally, parents should solicit the child's perspective as to what might be done to address the situation. Considering the emotional state of the child or teen, how much harm has taken place, and how much bullying might continue will also help parents to determine whether specific responses are sufficient or if more intervention should occur.

Similarly, the aggressor needs to be counseled by her parents in order to elicit an appropriate amount of remorse and guilt. If the bully does not feel these emotions immediately, professional help may be needed to treat underlying pathology of the victimizer. Parents will need help if this is the case; they will need professional mental-health support in discussing with their child how cyberbullying affects others and how to work toward cultivating empathy.

What Busy Parents Should Do If Their Child Is Cyberbullied

1. Make sure their child is, and remains, safe.
2. Solicit their child's perspective as to what he would like to see happen.
3. Collect evidence.

4. Keep detailed records of what happened, where it happened, and who else might have witnessed the incident(s).
5. Contact the school to make them aware of the situation.
6. Contact the service provider or content provider.
7. Contact the police if physical threats, stalking, coercion, blackmail, or sexually explicit pictures or videos of minors are involved.
8. Express to their child how important it is not to retaliate. (Hinduja and Patchin, 2015, 208)

Overall, busy parents need to demonstrate to their children and teens—through words and actions—that the situation needn't become even more egregious. This can be accomplished by working together to arrive at a mutually agreeable course of action using Parental Intelligence (see next chapter). Targeted youth need to realize they are not to blame and that no one deserves to be harassed in any environment. Teens need to know that their busy parents are not dismissive of what they are experiencing and how they are being harmed.

Apart from these response options, children and teens need to learn strategies that re-empower them if they are threatened. For example, teens may consider adjusting their account or privacy settings to block or regulate the content that they receive or are exposed to. They need to be reminded that they should be in control of their online experiences—to the extent they can. They needn't feel socially obligated to keep from unfriending or unfollowing those they don't feel a sense of safety with. It's important for parents to learn the proper settings to delete, block, filter, and report certain people and content on social media so that they can help their teen when necessary. Even busy parents know that it's well worth the time and effort spent in the long run.

Hinduja and Patchin make a final important point:

> We certainly do not want to trivialize any instance of cyberbullying and would encourage teens to seek help in addressing those [instances] they perceive as serious. However, it bears repeating that they should do all they can to keep from dwelling on hurtful words they know are false and only said to inflame emotions and promote controversy, conflict, and drama. This is an acquired skill, to be sure, and even as adults we do not always perceive and respond to sarcastic, mean, or hateful comments in the most productive way. Cultivating resiliency is vital to relational success in adulthood—which is chock full of interpersonal challenges; and perhaps youth (with the

help of involved teachers and parents) can use the more minor instances of cyberbullying as life lessons in that regard. (2015, 213, 214)

CHAPTER FIVE

THE PARENTAL INTELLIGENCE WAY

Behavior carries a message. It's not a solo act. It is an invitation for understanding.

While individual parents all face unique challenges, I have discovered many commonalities that affect their varied situations. To teach parenting effectively, I have developed five powerfully valuable steps that allow busy parents—no matter how different their circumstances—to find meaning behind their child's technological behavior and, beyond that, to intelligently and compassionately resolve the underlying problems.

The five steps to Parental Intelligence elaborated in Hollman's *Unlocking Parental Intelligence: Finding Meaning in Your Child's Behavior* (2015) are:

1. Stepping Back
2. Self-Reflecting
3. Understanding Your Child's Mind
4. Understanding Your Child's Development
5. Problem Solving

Together, these five steps provide a road map to help you get to your destination: the place where you understand the meaning behind your child's behavior. What was once obscure will become clear. When the meaning or meanings behind a behavior are understood, it is much easier to decide the best ways to handle a situation. Although the unfolding steps are described in sequence, it is valuable to go back and forth among them as you unlock your Parental Intelligence. Especially when handling the problem-solving step, self-reflecting and understanding your child's mind are often repeated. As new information comes to light, empathy between you and your child will deepen. Going through the five-step process with your child often uncovers problems that are of greater significance than the original behavior. What had been unspeakable will become known, and a new and stronger alliance will form between you and your child.

STEP ONE
Stepping Back

A parent's first reaction to misbehavior by or toward their child or teen is often emotional. Without distancing themselves from their emotional response, busy parents often make rash decisions, leading to punishments or actions that they later regret because the desired result is not achieved. Responding effectively means starting from the same emotional place each time. This may be uncomfortable, but making it a priority to step back, tolerate your child's feelings, and shift to a more reasoned response will lead to a better outcome.

Imagine taking a video of your child's behavior, rewinding it, and playing it back in slow motion to get a more detailed picture of what occurred. This means tracking the behavior and giving it a beginning, middle, and end. Thinking this way allows you to recall what happened before the incident—what your child did, what was done to your child, what you did, and how you felt. While having information doesn't mean you know what to do with it, it does set the stage for more enlightened parenting choices in the future.

Stepping back requires opening up your thinking and allowing yourself to experience a wide range of emotions without taking immediate action. Sometimes, after an incident, busy parents feel anxious, on edge, and restless, and they immediately jump into action to alleviate these feelings. Other times, busy parents refrain from acting impulsively but feel a nagging tension that interferes with their ability to see the situation objectively. Such a parent may be stuck in one point of view or focus solely on a specific—but incomplete—set of details. It is not always enough to replay an event, because the replay may confirm or intensify the original emotion. For stepping back to be effective, a busy parent must replay the event while also trying to understand the original emotions the event provoked in him or her.

The process of stepping back also includes the suspension of judgment. This allows you to take time to figure out what happened before taking action. If you never pause, you never allow emotions to subside and thinking to begin. Stepping back prepares you to engage in the parenting mind-set that says: what happened is meaningful. Even in an emergency, once the immediate situation has been handled, there is room for refraining from ready conclusions and for stepping back. Some people primarily look inward and tend to think things through. But not all thinking is productive reasoning; without sufficient information, your thoughts might well be going in circles. A parent may be reluctant to review and rethink her original reaction, fearing she will appear soft, inadequate, or inconsistent. Other parents are primarily outwardly directed and focus on what is going on around them—excluding their own and their child's inner feelings and thoughts when they are trying to understand their child's misbehavior. There may be a reluctance to go inside oneself to experience emotions, for fear of feeling out of control.

Stepping back requires slowing down and thinking about what just happened and how you feel about it, suspending not only judgment about your child's behavior but also about your parenting behavior.

Stepping back gives the parent permission to not always know what to do. Consequently, when a parent reacts one way on the spot, but later understands what happened more fully, he can feel confident returning to the child with new thoughts and feelings. Though these feelings were once restricted, they begin to expand and offer a new perspective. When you step back, you prepare yourself to recognize that behaviors have many causes. By pausing, you give yourself time to compare the last time the behavior happened to the present situation. You may discover a pattern in your interaction with your child and begin to wonder, *Are there any causes for this behavior that I couldn't consider last time?* You may then begin to see the behavior in its many aspects: What triggered the behavior? How long did it last? When did it escalate or decrease? You may also begin to see facets of the behavior—facets you were once blind to because of the high emotional states during the incident. Once you are focused on seeking a full knowledge of what happened, you will begin to discover that several problems might be involved in the misbehavior. Once you calm down, you begin to notice expressions on your child's face, the words your child said, your child's gestures and postures, and your child's mood and shifts in feelings. After a while, this one behavior can be broken down and understood as many separate behaviors.

Stepping back can open up your mind to such an extent that you may feel you're observing a different behavior or group of behaviors than what you did originally. Stepping back gives you space and time to evaluate the situation, examine and question assumptions, and realize that the situation isn't fully understood.

Take as much time as you need to consider what is happening. In your mind, say to yourself, *Slo-o-o-w down. Take your time. Hold on. Don't thrust forward. Resist those impulses. Breathe deeply. Sit quietly. Consider what to say or do, if anything.*

Both mothers and fathers who are invested in the *process*—not just the outcomes—of child rearing have a greater tendency to naturally learn to step back. Fathers and mothers can encourage and help each other in stepping back, particularly in two-parent households where co-parenting is a goal. Parents who live in separate residences but share in co-parenting can also help each other to step back. They can find good alternatives to impulsive reactions as they learn how to balance their responsibilities for both work and childcare—and then share their insights with each other. The significance of mothers and fathers supporting each other in the process of stepping back cannot be underestimated. A mother may be the buffer to a father's automatic release of anger, just as he may do the same for her.

When you give yourself permission to slow down before reacting and deciding on consequences, you can reduce stress and feel more in control. Stepping back changes the tone between parent and child. When children see their parents taking their time, they start to feel—perhaps cautiously at first—that their parents can be trusted to guide them. Here is an example: A ten-year-old was playing his video games for two hours rather than doing his homework, which was his usual routine. His mother felt frustrated and angry and felt like bursting into his room to yell at him to get to work. Instead, she calmed herself and stepped back to consider how unusual her son's behavior was—maybe it had some meaning. This pause helped her to control her emotions so that, after only a few minutes, she could knock on her son's door and ask to come in and talk. To her surprise she found out that her son's school had declared a no-homework day in order to give their pressured kids a break; and that's why he was enjoying his video games. Fortunately, because she stepped back, the mother did not rashly scream at her son and start a brouhaha for no reason!

Summary of Stepping Back

The purpose of stepping back is to set the stage for parents to take stock of their feelings and organize their thinking about what has just occurred or is occurring. This is just common sense, but it requires tolerating frustration—a skill we are hoping to also teach our children. While thinking over what occurred, parents ideally suspend judgment and acknowledge that misbehavior carries meaning. This first step in the Parental Intelligence parenting approach helps parents to embrace the concept that the behavior communicates a child's feelings and motives and may indicate problems that need to be solved in the parent-child relationship.

The next step, self-reflecting, increases a parent's ability to understand his own feelings, motives, and reactions concerning a child's puzzling behavior.

STEP TWO
Self-Reflecting

Self-reflecting allows you to discover how your past affects your present approach to parenting. Self-reflecting allows you to observe yourself objectively and think about the genesis of your feelings, motives, and actions in both present and previous relationships. This step requires honestly questioning *why* you behaved the way you did, as the parent. Sounds logical, but I know it can be hard. It's so tempting to just jump to ready solutions and skip questioning what's going on inside of you.

For parents, self-reflecting is an extension of stepping back. It requires you to consider what led to your specific responses to your child's behavior (or your child's response to another's behavior toward them), prompts you to think about your actions from many perspectives, and allows you to consider many causes for your responses. That sounds like a tall order, but if you take it bit by bit, you will be amazed at what you discover. Self-reflecting happens after the incident of your child's misbehavior—maybe hours or days later. Sometimes it is subtle. You may be in your car at a red light, and your mind returns to the situation. By considering your reactions, you may suddenly see them from a different perspective. You discuss the situation—and specifically your reactions—with a friend or a spouse, and they offer new perspectives on your reactions. Other times you may purposefully rethink the problem behavior and ask yourself if there are other ways to approach the situation or if you could mirror the ways you've seen other parents react to similar situations. You begin to question, *Why did I react that particular way, now that I see it wasn't the only way?* or *What were my motives and intentions?* or *What in my past affected my thinking and actions in the present?* or *What were my emotional reactions to my child's behavior, and where did they come from?*

If you allow yourself to take your time, this isn't as difficult as you might imagine. In fact, you may notice that you feel more confident as you strive to look inward. Self-reflecting is a discovery process. You are getting to know yourself better. It feels good. Self-reflecting allows you to learn more about yourself as a child and teenager and about the effect your experiences may have had on your present reactions to your child.

Self-reflecting often leads to a realization that you take your child's actions very personally. That's hard to accept, but it's also relieving to understand. You may realize that sometimes you feel persecuted by your child; you want to be the boss, yet your child has control. Then you reflect further and consider how to be authoritative, yet kind and compassionately involved in your child's life. This takes a strong sense of self—a capacity for self-awareness. Practicing this self-awareness can help you to feel better about yourself.

Your relationships with your own caregivers—which may include parents, teachers, and other adults—during infancy, childhood, and adolescence may determine your capacity for reflective functioning as an adult. Your early experiences shape the expectations of future attachments. When you strive to bring your own conflicts from the past to the forefront of your mind and understand them, it can help you to help your child. Admittedly, patterns of relationships are often unconscious and difficult to change without therapeutic intervention. Nonetheless, even if parents seek treatment, they can't just wait for their therapy to end before helping their child; their child continues to grow and needs help now. It can be surprisingly effective for busy parents to realize that their thoughts and reactions can come from the past and may affect the specific behavior in question.

Think of a distressing behavior your child exhibits. Consider your feelings during the incident. Now go back and find a past experience that triggered the same or similar feelings. Review the experience slowly, like a story, in as much detail as you can. Think about the people in your life at that time and what they meant to you, then and now. You may find that your child's present behavior triggers aspects from that past situation. Ask yourself some questions: *Does my child's behavior remind me of my behavior in the past? Does my child's behavior remind me of someone else's behavior in the past? Was my past situation a marker for me in some way? Was the past situation a turning point in my life? Do I have unresolved feelings about that time?* As you go through this mental and emotional process, you may begin remembering more and more. Thoughts and details that were hidden for years may begin to surface. All of these memories may very well have to do with the way you now react to your child.

There are several possibilities. If your child's behavior, manner, posture, or tone of voice resonates with how you interacted with someone else at earlier times in your life, you may be reacting to your child the way you reacted when you were younger. This can be very enlightening. Or you may be reacting to your child the way you wished you had reacted when you were younger. Have you had any epiphanies? Are light bulbs going off? If your mind is racing backward, you may be feeling much more in touch with your reactions. Alternatively, your reaction to your child's behavior may be occurring because someone once reacted to you the way your child is behaving now. This may be very upsetting to you. As past and present have converged, it's no wonder you react so strongly.

Here's an example: A thirteen-year-old girl was online and texting her friends all afternoon. Even though her homework was done, her mother thought she should be reading or engaging in a face-to-face activity with some friends, not just staying on her phone or computer. Stepping back, the mother's mind began to wander back to when she was thirteen and she and her mother argued almost all the time. She remembered thinking that her mother never understood her social needs; they were at odds so much of the time. Remembering that relationship, the mother realized that she didn't want to have the same connection with her teen. So instead of acting annoyed quickly, she began chatting with her daughter about her friends at school and her current social life. To her surprise, her daughter was very willing to open up and they had a great discussion about her social pressures. The mother was so relieved to have a better kind of mother-daughter responsivity than she'd had with her mother. She was overjoyed and so glad that she self-reflected.

Your capacity for self-reflection may grow as your child grows. If your child reaches an age that was troublesome for you when you were young, conflict between you and your child may ensue because you are reminded of your unresolved problems at that age. However, realizing that you dealt with similar issues can open up your understanding by leaps and bounds. It may take a lifetime to become adept at self-reflecting, but as you're learning, you can improve your relationship with your child.

There are many past stereotypes about women being more empathic and tuned-in to feelings than men are, which you might think would affect a man's capacity to self-reflect. However, in thirty years of experience with many different parents, I have not seen either gender self-reflecting more than the other. I have, however, found that men's past experiences with their fathers when they were children affects what they expect of themselves as fathers. Men either want to give their children the same positive experiences they had with their fathers, or they want to give their children better fathering experiences than they had. Both women and men whose fathers were not active in their lives may have low expectations for the father's involvement with their children.

Women with such low expectations may be surprised and pleased when their children's fathers want to be invested in parenting. Or, this may have been part of what attracted them to these men. Similarly, women may look back at their mothers' involvement with them as children as something they want to emulate or change when they become mothers. When parents engage in self-reflecting, these yearnings come to light and can have a positive effect on their children.

Summary of Self-Reflecting

As parents understand themselves better through self-reflecting, they become more consciously aware of the impact their past has on their present responses to their children in specific situations. As a result, punishment can recede into the background and parents can discover alternative reactions that are far more effective at handling a specific singular transgression. Parental self-reflecting leads to new levels of compassion and resilience in parent-child relationships. Stepping back and self-reflecting add great depth to understanding your current reactions to your child.

Self-reflecting helps mothers and fathers question why they react in punitive ways instead of searching for meaning. In time, parental impulsive reactions that lead to punishment wane, creating a readiness for flexible, sensitized decision-making. Insightful decision-making builds a bridge to your child that leads to understanding your child's mind—step three in this parenting approach.

STEP THREE
Understanding Your Child's Mind

"What's on your mind?" is a question often asked casually, but understanding your child's mind is central to knowing your child. This casual question prompts a series of other questions about parenting. Does understanding the mind of a child help the child cope? Does understanding the mind of a child help you cope? And what roles do emotions play in your child's thinking?

Understanding your child's mind starts with knowing your child's mental states. What are they? The term *mental state* refers to all mental experiences. A short list of mental states would include intentions, thoughts, desires, wishes, beliefs, and feelings. Additionally, it's important to understand that contradictory and diverse mental states can occur at the same time. For example, a teen wishes (a mental state) to have ice cream, and yet he feels he shouldn't because he intends (a mental state) to lose weight so he can make the wrestling team.

When I talk about mental states, I am also referring to physical states, because they are inextricably interwoven. This can be especially seen in adolescence. A teen has a mind with feelings and desires. How does the attentive mother notice these mental states? When the teen feels self-doubt (a mental state), he may withdraw to his room. The mother knows not to chase after him and then observes contentment (another mental state) when the teen reappears and wants to chat. Your ability to understand your child's mind is directly related to your ability to self-reflect. As described above, self-reflecting is your capacity to think about your own past experiences. Self-awareness and awareness of the mental states of others are closely linked. When, with self-reflecting, you are able to understand how your own mind is working, you also realize that your child's mind is separate and autonomous from yours. However, if you do not understand this, you may attribute your own mental states (intentions and feelings) to your child and her misbehaviors.

For example, let's say you are angry at your ten-year-old for being curt with you. It's breakfast time, and you laid out a balanced, delicious meal for him on the kitchen table: toast with his favorite jam, granola, and his favorite fruit-juice smoothie—the works! However, he barely says "good morning" while holding onto his phone, and then grabs a piece of toast and runs out the door. You feel disrespected. He barely noticed what you'd done and you're angry he wasn't grateful for the lovely meal you prepared. You then assume he was mad at you from the quick, "See ya," he called without even looking at you. His anger was completely unjustified and the assumption is simple: you're angry; he's angry. You've forgotten that your child's feelings and intentions may be quite different from your own. In this example, your child may have simply been curt because he was running late for the school bus. In fact, you may find out after school when you talk that he was in a hurry because his old printer was on the blink and he couldn't fix it, making it impossible for him to print his homework. After figuring out that the printer needed a new ink cartridge, he had been able to print out his homework but had felt very rushed. That's why he was so quick during breakfast—he was in a hurry and wasn't mad at you at all.

Here's another example: A teen is frustrated when the dinner in a restaurant isn't served quickly and complains vigorously that she's starving. She keeps looking at her phone and writing texts to her friends to distract herself from her hunger. Her father, however, had a big lunch, is enjoying everyone's company, and doesn't mind waiting. He finds his fifteen-year-old daughter's complaints rude and scolds her, telling her to quiet down and put away her phone or she can't go out later.

The daughter feels resentful. The father and daughter's mental states—their intentions and feelings—are different. This girl's father mistakenly assumed that what was on his mind is also on his daughter's mind. An inability to be aware that your own mental state is different from that of your child can lead to a misinterpretation of the intent of your child's behavior. This causes a rupture in the parent-child relationship and, sometimes, unnecessary punishment. Understanding your child's mind depends on realizing the links between intentions, feelings, thoughts, and behaviors, and looking for meanings behind behaviors. Behaviors and feelings are inextricably bound together.

For instance, a mother might say to her son, "You punched the wall when your brother interrupted your video game. He's been doing this for weeks, and your frustration has reached its limit. Think about it. I bet by hitting the wall, you were avoiding hitting him." Now that she's planted a new idea in her son's mind, she continues, "Let's think and talk more about your frustration, so you don't ever need to punch a wall." She's now connected his emotion—frustration—to his behavior—punching.

Busy parents who approach situations like this mother are attuned to what's going on in their child's mind and, in turn, what caused the behavior. While the father in the example at the restaurant was unable to shift from a punitive stance to understanding his child's mind, this mother linked her son's internal emotional state to his behavior.

Most parents and children can recognize each other's moods but need time to figure out the reason for a particular mood. Behavior is meaningful, even if you don't catch on right away. Often, you need to let the behavior sit in your mind and wait for its meaning to emerge. This is stepping back. If, as a busy parent, you know your child very well and have been trying to understand his or her mind for many years and over many developmental stages, you can become quite an expert at reading your child's moods and thoughts.

Of course, it's important to check your ideas with your child. This shows empathy: "It seems like your teacher hurt your feelings, so you bolted out of the classroom. Was it something like that?" Let's say your child then reveals that, yes, she is feeling hurt. After hearing your child's response, you might continue: "Now that we figured out what was going on in your mind, were there other choices you may have had that would be a better way to react the next time you feel hurt?"

No one likes being instructed on how they should feel, but it sure feels good to be understood. Everyone appreciates empathy, and feeling understood can help a child contain his emotions and begin to think them through. When a child feels his parent understands what is going on inside his mind, he feels attended to and supported, and then can think further about how to handle situations.

It's important to realize, however, that all parents had experiences growing up that caused the formation of emotional triggers that still exist in the present—often unconsciously. These triggers prompt responses to their children's behaviors, and they are very hard to unlearn. This can interfere with empathy. Thus, early emotional triggers in the parent may lead to misinterpretations of what is actually leading to a child's particular behavior. This can be resolved by returning to further self-reflecting, and then empathy can resume.

What does understanding your child's mind have to do with empathy? Understanding your child's mind is part of empathy—understanding the emotional states of another person. For example, parents form an idea of what their child might be feeling when they see a particular emotional expression on her face. It's like trying to step into your child's shoes and see from her point of view.

Understanding your child's mind in this way is a creative act. However, it is an act of imagination with severe limitations: no one can know another person's mind with complete accuracy. Thus, it is best to approach the task by asking questions rather than by making statements.

This empathic approach can be difficult if you did not have parents who modeled empathy. If you had caretakers in your life who didn't empathize with your needs and emotions and who didn't explore how people's behaviors impacted others, empathizing with your own children will most likely not come naturally. So, give yourself time to catch on to your child's feelings. It's remarkable how good it feels when you understand something new about your child. You know you've done well when your son or daughter says, "Hey, Mommy. You really get it. Thanks."

Empathic parents tend to raise empathic children. They become interested in how their parents think and feel and may be quite good listeners. As your child learns that he can look to you to understand his states of mind (intentions, feelings, beliefs), he may become interested in understanding your states of mind. It's not that roles should be reversed, where the child becomes the listener to the parents' problems, but it does mean that an empathic child will want to understand where his parents (and other people around him) are coming from. In order to understand your child's mind, it helps to be a good observer. Verbal communication is only one piece of the puzzle. Watch your child's facial expressions to get an idea of what's on his mind.

All of these expressions indicate various emotions. Here are some examples described by Paul Ekman (2007) in his book *Emotions Revealed*: a furrowed brow (worry or anger), raised eyebrows and lips in the shape of an "O" (surprise), a twitching eye (anxiety), crinkled lines at the edge of the eyes (anger), glazed-over eyes (detachment), a wrinkled nose (annoyance), and pursed lips (fury). Speech, of course, helps us understand another's mind, but silences, stiffening or relaxation of muscles, and facial expressions are also meaningful. Because facial language is so important, parents are advised to refrain from saying, "Get that sneer off your face," or, "Don't roll your eyes at me" when they are angry; this can lead to the child hiding or masking expressions that are so essential to understanding what is on his mind. Even before they can talk, young children are interpreting our facial expressions; so while you are interpreting your child's expressions, your child is doing the same with yours.

Body language also indicates what's on your child's mind. Finger pointing or folded arms suggest anger. A droopy head suggests hopelessness. Foot shaking suggests nervous energy. Averting one's head or turning one's back may mean anger or avoidance. When your child suddenly stands up when you are sitting together, fury may be the cause; alternatively, standing may be the prelude to giving up and walking away. The better you know your child, the better you will be at interpreting your observations.

Sometimes we are blind to an emotion in our children that we block out in ourselves. For instance, an angry parent who blocks out hurt is blind to his child's hurt. Thus, parents can misperceive what they feel, thinking they feel only one emotion (anger) while truly feeling something else (hurt). If this is true, then recognizing your child's hurt might lead to you feeling your own. If you don't know what is on your own mind— what you are thinking and feeling—you may subsequently be blocked from understanding what is on your child's mind—what she is thinking and feeling. You may draw erroneous conclusions and rashly punish. It's helpful if you understand that mental states are changeable, that they affect behavior, and that understanding them leads to stronger parent-child relationships.

If both mother and father are involved in their children's daily lives, the diverse interpretations of their parental communications make children feel listened to and understood. The mother or father don't always have to immediately catch on to what their child is trying to get across. This takes time. It is the parents' efforts that matters. Children become more confident when both parents value their ideas and feelings. At the same time, parents can discover that their children are more capable than they knew as they learn the meanings behind their kids' behaviors. Mothers and fathers may understand their infants', children's, and teens' minds differently by interpreting behaviors, sounds, words, gestures, facial expressions, and other body language in different ways. However, what matters most is that both parents are interested in what goes on in their child's mind and how their child's mind works. Parental Intelligence highlights the immense importance of this type of maternal and paternal involvement.

Summary of Understanding Your Child's Mind

Trying to understand your child's mind is essential for knowing who she is and how she thinks and feels. If busy parents want to change their child's behavior, they need to learn about their child's mental states. What is on the parent's mind affects what is on the child's mind— and vice versa. Parents who have their child's mind in mind are more likely to have children who are self-reflective and secure. Busy parents who are able to think about their children's minds manage their parent-child relationships better and are more effective in resolving inevitable conflicts and arguments.

Trying to understand your children's minds shows them you believe in them and teaches them to believe in themselves. Treating your children like capable human beings with well-functioning minds and good intentions builds trust.

STEP FOUR
Understanding Your Child's Development

There are developmental stages at which children master different skills, but not all children reach those stages at the same time. For example, your seven-year-old may be more adept at completing a math problem than a nine-year-old. Your thirteen-year-old may be more empathic than a sixteen-year-old. Two children in the same grade may perform differently on the same assignment. Have you noticed that when your firstborn was a teen, she had great problem-solving skills and a high level of frustration tolerance, while your next-in-line was pretty inflexible and had trouble handling frustration as a teen?

The age when a child reaches a certain skill level is the child's *developmental age* for that skill, regardless of the child's chronological age. When parents take into account the developmental age of their child—which reflects the stage the child has reached in mastering certain capacities—parents and children get along better. What capacities should you look for? Notice your child's interpersonal skills: impulse control, effective communication, and empathy. Other skills include thinking or cognition. Watch for the development of individual capacities, such as autonomy and identity formation. You'll probably find your children aren't consistent across the board, but they have strengths and weaknesses. The chronological age may not be the same as the developmental age for any of these capacities, and children may be at different developmental levels for different skills. When you set expectations for your children, be sure they reflect each child's developmental levels, which may fall behind or step ahead of their chronological age.

It helps to ask two questions: "What is expected at my child's stage of development?" and "How far apart is my child's chronological age from my child's developmental age?" Punishing or being critical of a child for not completing tasks expected for their chronological age creates problems that affect your relationship. Expectations that do not reflect your child's developmental age won't be met and will create acute emotional distress. This is especially true for a child with delays or disabilities that prevent him from reaching the general milestones of that age.

Once you have taken the earlier steps by stepping back, self-reflecting, and understanding your child's mind, understanding your child's developmental stage becomes essential for effective problem solving. Mothers and fathers should also be aware of their own physical and emotional changes during their child's development that may affect their readiness to understand the stages their child is going through.

Here is a list of developmental goals that can be aspired to as your child matures, listed with increasing complexity:

- Working toward high standards of behavior
- Developing morality
- Learning limits
- Tolerating frustration and disappointment
- Developing resilience and flexibility
- Cultivating empathy
- Encouraging multi-causal thinking
- Sustaining curiosity and persistence
- Becoming responsible
- Forming positive, long-lasting parent-child and friend relationships

It's important to understand both why children should learn to accept limits and tolerate hearing "no" and how parents struggle with these goals. Have you ever had the frustrating feeling that no one is listening to you when you say "no"? You try to speak firmly but find yourself asking a question instead of making a statement. You hear yourself asking, "Will you brush your teeth now?" But what you want to say is, "Brush your teeth this minute!" Then you find yourself screaming, and your child is crying. What went wrong? Parents often lack the confidence to make clear statements firmly—though kindly—when they are not quite sure how their children will react. When you understand that your expectations are reasonable, you can make that firm statement, "Please brush your teeth now," and follow through.

So, let's look at when children can receive a "no" and give one themselves. From early infancy, children learn that parents set limits on their behaviors. After a certain time set by the parent, a baby slowly learns to sleep more at night than during the day. Eventually, the baby sleeps through the night with naps during the day. Thus, the baby learns to adapt to the wake-sleep cycle expected in her culture. The baby learns that there are limits to how her needs are satisfied and that the parent can and will say "no."

By age two, the child is experimenting with some newfound autonomy, developing his own ability to say "no." Over time, this child develops a further understanding of others saying, "No, not now, later." This requires the ability to wait, to tolerate frustration, and to become flexible. As the months and years progress, children develop this capacity more fully, although it fluctuates depending on their state of mind at a given moment. For example, a calm child without too many stressors can tolerate frustration more easily than a child in a high-stress family situation. However, it is more complex than focusing only on external stressors. There are internal stressors as well: a predisposition to anxiety, a sensitive temperament, and sensory processing abilities (how the child takes in sensory data visually, aurally, and kinesthetically and how the child processes or understands it), to name just a few factors. There is a developmental line for the ability to tolerate limits; this ability emerges and becomes stronger over time. If limits are not set for a young child, they feel too powerful and may try to control the adult. This is not good for them, because it is overwhelming to feel that your parent is not in control. When you feel self-doubt about being firm with everyday rules, remind yourself that you are helping your child by giving her the security of clear expectations—which organize her inner and outer world.

By adolescence, the child is developing a new sense of identity and autonomy. Limits are being tested regularly as the teenager finds his way to define himself in the world of peers and adults. The child who could tolerate limits effectively earlier in life has a less difficult time during teenage years. The child who has not mastered this capacity sufficiently struggles when faced with restrictions and rules appropriate to his age.

It is important even for the teenager to know that there are limits to how she satisfies her needs so that she doesn't feel too powerful and out of control. Reasonable rules and restrictions help the teen eventually develop an understanding about what she wants and what is expected of her. Although this may be frustrating, it is actually calming, because the teen then knows what is expected, when to do things, and how to respond. The push and pull between teen and parent at this stage helps the teen define herself. Teenagers rebel less often when they know their parents' motives are clear and positive. When adolescents know their parents have cared about them in the past by trying to understand their vantage points, they become good decision-makers, following their own values even when surrounded by peer pressure. There is less pushback when teenagers know that their parents have concern for their welfare and well-being and that setting limits comes out of love.

It is interesting that the parent is also learning to define himself as a parent at his adolescent's stage of development. Parents go through developmental passages in their parenting life—along with their children—that pertain to limit setting. For instance, some parents are more comfortable setting limits with babies and toddlers than tweens and teens and vice versa. Often this has to do with unresolved earlier stages of the parent's developmental life. For example, if a parent had a troubling adolescence that had not been understood, when his child reaches adolescence it might be harder for that parent to understand the changes his teen is experiencing—and thus understand realistic limit setting.

For different parents at different times in their parenting life, it may be necessary to return to self-reflection before understanding what to expect of their child at specific stages of development. Then they can become confident in setting reasonable limits that their child accepts.

Summary of Understanding Your Child's Development

Parents who understand and nurture their child's development can more effectively evaluate what they can expect of their child. Misbehaviors become signals of a child's developmental stage or of a child's need for meaningful communication. The child is not viewed as "bad" but rather as distressed and in need of help clarifying her motivations and intentions. Rules can be devised, limits can be set, and achievements can be expected that fit the child's developmental age. Consequently, children can comprehend limits, tolerate frustration, be empathic of others, and form rich, enduring parent-child and peer relationships.

STEP FIVE
Problem Solving

The more you continue working on the first four steps, the more natural and effective they will become, getting you ready for the last step—problem solving. Interestingly, after working through the first four steps, the initial problem—a specific behavior—has become part of a set of problems to be solved over time. The immediate importance of the initial behavior may have lessened because it has been recognized as a symptom of more pressing issues lying underneath. These are the problems you ultimately hope to solve, together with your child, using Parental Intelligence.

The steps in this book that lead to problem solving are based on your desire to have a strong, healthy, and joyful relationship with your child. It is usually possible to repair a relationship, even if it has been ruptured in past conflicts. The key to repairing a ruptured relationship is a secure, trusting relationship. Without a good relationship, problems are rarely solved.

The steps leading from stepping back to problem solving seem linear, but you may need to go back and forth among them. This is truly significant because the earlier steps, or lack thereof, directly affect the process of problem solving. If, for example, you attempt to talk with your child and problem solve, but then the conversation slips back into blaming by either you or your child, it is time to go back to earlier steps. If, as another example, you or your child consider each other's behavior to be intentionally oppositional, authoritarian, or a power struggle, then, again, it is important to go back to earlier steps. Or if, during problem solving, you find that you or your child's voice is tinged with sarcasm, you may be off track; a new problem may have surfaced, signaled by the sarcasm. Address that issue first, and use your new skills (e.g., understanding your child's mind) to identify what is driving your child to speak that way to you. If you find you are becoming sarcastic, angry, or more jittery and irritable than usual, use your new skills (e.g., stepping back) to reflect on potential triggers. In each of these instances, taking a break from problem solving to figure out your own and your child's reactions will be worth the effort.

While problem solving, you may realize you need to be more reflective about your view of reality and your child's view of reality. If, indeed, you and your child can see the problem from each other's points of view, both you and your child should be ready to problem solve together.

Let's think more about points of view. It is worth revisiting self-reflecting at this point. Maybe you suddenly realize that your child's view of an experience is similar to one you held as a child, too. This sudden realization gives you pause and helps you better understand both your child and yourself. You also realize that you were resistant to understanding your child in the first place because your child provoked the past in you, something you did not want to remember. Re-experiencing past emotions and events can have the benefit of allowing you to rethink the present event. You can then better understand where your child is coming from and solve the problem together. Sometimes the problem that needs to be addressed isn't an event or misbehavior, but instead is the way you communicate with your child. When you realize your reactions came from the past, your interactions become increasingly empathic.

In other words, for problem solving to become possible and effective, you need to try to understand what is on both your mind and your child's mind. You need to view the situation not only from your point of view but also from your child's vantage point. If you can do so and share your understanding with your child, your child will be prompted to reciprocate. If you can't comprehend and picture your child's reality, you can't solve a problem with him.

Your child, too, needs to try to understand your view of the problem. If both of you can't embrace the other's point of view of the problem, you both must sort that out before advancing to solving the problem at hand. Problem solving also needs to take into account your child's developmental stage, which allows you to understand your child's actual capabilities and skill set relevant to the problem.

Communication through speech, gestures, and facial expressions are affected by moods and temperaments. We all know how variable moods can be from moment to moment or day to day. Communication is not always smooth when problem solving; it can be awkward and uncertain. If you and your child expect there may be many uncomfortable moments, they won't deter you from continuing to pursue the step of problem solving. Problem solving aims to find mutual meanings, which may be new to both participants. Meanings are exchanged through taking collaborative turns in talking things out in order to correct misinterpretations of the behavior in question.

The benefits are numerous. Both parents and children are more effective as they repair their differences and develop a positive feeling about their relationship with each other. Parent and child learn new coping skills that can be used in the future, which fosters optimism for future interactions. Problem solving takes time, but for busy parents these steps gives them a structure they can depend on and come back to when they have more time. Sticking with it and being persistent can be difficult. Also, like any plan, it's only a good one if it is carried out. Remember that it took a long time for the problems between you and your child to build up; it will also take time to repair them. The busy parent can explain that to their child and make a plan for when and how they find time to problem solve. The challenge is to hold on to your belief that the relationship can be salvaged, and the problems can be resolved. Without this commitment, things can fall apart quickly. When your child sees that your commitment is loving and genuine, she will feel deeply cared for and persist as well. When both you and your child are determined to use your energy to make problem solving work, it is highly likely that things will work out to everyone's benefit.

The structure of the family has been changing in recent decades. For example, current trends suggest that both mothers and fathers feel conflicted about time spent away from family and struggle to maintain balance between working outside the home—often for very long hours—and spending time with their children. Although either or both parents work outside the home, they spend more time with their children than parents did in the past. This gives mothers and fathers more opportunities to be devoted to carrying out the step of problem solving with their children. For children, problem solving is a developmental process and skill. Reciprocal interactions drive interpersonal development. When you, as the parent, engage in this process, you will find you are developing a collaborative relationship with your child. The ability to do this will rest on the mother-child and father-child relationships that have been growing as you accomplished the earlier steps of Parental Intelligence.

During problem solving, you will engage in a give-and-take between you and your child. Problem solving is a relational process. When children learn that their parents realize the underlying problems behind the original behavior, they become more open than ever to hearing what their parents have to say. This is because they are feeling understood.

Children are relieved to know their mother or father is open to their points of view, wants to hear about their feelings, and is aware of the developmental struggles they may be going through. In turn, as a parent feels the reciprocity of the open dialogue with their child, he slowly relaxes and trusts the open, honest, and empathic communication.

In the best possible world, each parent uses Parental Intelligence and is open to reciprocal communication. If not, problem solving will be most productive only with the parent who has followed the prior steps fully.

Summary of Problem Solving

Problem solving may appear to be the single most important step. To problem solve well, however, the earlier steps are just as—if not more—important. Because without these steps, you may not know what the most essential problems really are.

Parental Intelligence is a relationship-based approach to rearing children as opposed to solving problems by punishment. Parents don't lose their say about their children's behaviors, but rather they understand the reasons behind the behavior, its context, and workable approaches that help their children and themselves to change the behavior or their view of the behavior.

Parents and children alike feel comfortable enough to bring their agendas to the table in the hopes of not only solving the immediate situation, but also being understood. The parents' purpose is not only to find the underlying meaning in the particular behavior, but also to help the child learn to be aware of feelings, engage in logical thinking, face challenging developmental passages, and include the art of discussion in relationships. As parents step back, reflect, understand their own and their children's minds, and learn about child development, the meaning behind behaviors becomes clearer, and the actual overarching problems can be solved. In a secure relationship, where parents and children engage each other in reciprocal ways, and where the concerns of both parent and child are taken into consideration, alternate means to solving problems arise.

In an insecure attachment, where the bonds are more tenuous, the work is much more difficult, since parent and child do not reciprocally engage or trust each other. Children may expect that their parents will not be sensitive to their emotional and social cues, and those children will not want to engage in discussions for that very reason. Parents may likewise expect that children will just turn them off and not want to engage in discussions. Therapeutic help may be needed to redress this distrust and shift the relationship into a more secure position. When it is time to problem solve, children and parents may slip into avoidance tactics. They may change the subject, move around, begin a round of keeping secrets, hide their feelings about the relationship, and generally find ways to interrupt the interaction. This is where empathy comes in. Parents may need to clearly point out that their children are avoiding the discussion and they hope to understand why. Similarly, the misbehavior that began this process may reappear, demonstrating that the parents may have begun to unintentionally avoid the problems that underlie the unwanted behavior. Parents also need to take into account that young children don't think or articulate as quickly as adults. Adults, therefore, need to allow for pauses and silences. Parents need to stop themselves from slipping into lectures and coaching before the child has a chance to absorb what is being discussed and let the child have her say. Adolescents, too, need to avoid lecturing their parents with broad "philosophies of life" that drive the conversation from the issues at hand.

In time, if parent and child engage with each other, focus on their relationships, empathize with each other, and especially if parents make it a priority to identify the meanings behind their child's behaviors, a new quality of interaction will come to life. Problems can and will be solved to mutual satisfaction. When this relationship is well-established, busy parents find they interact with their kids in more empathic ways and the element of time is not so much an issue. This is because parents and kids now trust each other to come back when they have more time to completely solve a problem. Having a five-step structure to rely on facilitates quick thinking and immediate or transitional problem resolution when parents and when kids are busy and on the run.

SUMMARY
Five Steps to Parental Intelligence

Through the evolving process of unlocking Parental Intelligence, each parent learns a great deal about their own mind and the mind of their child. That is, each parent accepts the challenge of learning what is going on inside himself if he is to discover what is going on inside his child.

Ruptures in a parent-child relationship cannot be avoided, but the continued experience of repair secures and strengthens the relationship. The child learns to trust the parent because she believes her parent is invested in understanding a vast array of emotions. Respect and trust are earned as pleasures are shared and problems are solved.

Different parents will have found some of the steps harder or easier to master, depending on the degree of empathy they already embraced as part of themselves before beginning the process. Each reader who has used the Parental Intelligence approach has learned how to decipher the meaning behind their child's behavior, only to find that there are overarching problems to be unmasked.

Becoming a meaning-maker is a profound experience that can change how you, as a parent, view children and teens and, most fundamentally, yourself. Parents who have unlocked their Parental Intelligence are introspective mothers and fathers who have become willing to understand and take a look at themselves in order to understand their children and know how they think. Parents learn not only what they and their children think about, but also how they carry out the thinking process.

Unlocking Parental Intelligence is a new stage of a mother or father's parenting life that will have lifelong results in how family members engage each other, care for each other, and view and solve problems over the long haul.

As we face the new generations that are immersed in technology, this collaborative approach becomes more important than ever before. Our children today expect to be heard, respected for their technological knowledge, and empathized with as they reciprocally empathize with their parents' state of technological knowledge. Earlier, I referred to the democratization of the family. The Parental Intelligence Way fits the bill.

CHAPTER SIX

CHILDREN AND TECHNOLOGY: THE PARENTAL INTELLIGENCE WAY

*B*usy parents question when they should allow their kids to have smartphones. Because both children and their parents are busy, parents like to be able to text their kids and know when and where they are going places. But parents also know that phone usage started too early can be addictive and lead to isolation; kids can feel isolated after using too much technology instead of socializing with their friends *in person*. Busy parents are practical yet wise enough to not risk the early onset of depression, discussed in earlier chapters, in their children and teens—who isolate themselves online when they do not contact or connect with others.

ARI AND HIS PARENTS: THE QUESTION OF PHONE USAGE AT AGE TEN

Ari is a reserved child who just turned ten; he is in the fifth grade and attending middle school. He tends to keep to himself, reading books avidly, playing video games, and building projects with his dad. He has a few friends but doesn't tend to gravitate to social experiences, such as team sports. He enjoys school, does well academically, and has joined a science club that meets two days after school. He's been pressing his parents for an iPhone, because he likes all the apps and music and looks forward to using them. He also enjoys photography and wants to be able to take pictures and create videos with his phone. On the school bus, he's noticed that all the other kids have phones, even those younger than he is, so he feels justified in pressing his parents to get him an up-to-date smartphone. He's tech-wise and knows he'll be able to go online with it as well as use it as an actual phone. His parents' main hesitation is their worry that Ari is so tech-wise that he'll isolate himself from making friends except through texting, iMessaging, and emailing. He doesn't have a penchant for FaceTime, but his parents would be pleased if he did; then he'd have more personal contact with others.

Ari's dad is an introverted guy and doesn't object to the phone, feeling that society's preference for extroverted people isn't the way of the world or necessary. People have different temperaments and personalities, and he feels that Ari is well-adjusted and a great kid. Ari's mother is more of a happy-go-lucky social person and worries about Ari isolating himself—even though he joined the science club, to her delight. She wants him to feel in the social loop and likes the idea of being able to contact him when she's at work. However, she and her husband are very busy professionals and Ari is an only child, so she is fearful of Ari becoming addicted to phone usage even though his plans for using it are very varied.

Ari's folks decide to use the Parental Intelligence Way to resolve this question, collaborating with Ari about the decision.

Step One: Stepping Back

Ari came home from school one afternoon in a cheerful mood. His babysitter greeted him with a snack, and he went about doing his homework, waiting for his parents to return from work. He hoped that "today was the day" he was going to insist on getting a phone. When his parents arrived home, he approached them immediately; in fact, he began more aggressively than he usually would, as he had researched—and was set on getting—the newest iPhone.

After Ari made his claim for the phone, his parents said they'd talk in a bit but wanted some time to settle in at home first. Ari was impatient but let it go. His parents wanted time to step back and review their feelings about the question, which they did. Dad was for it; Ari's mother was hesitant.

Step Two: Self-Reflecting

Ari's mother felt anxiety about her son becoming more isolated as he entered adolescence. She also knew her husband was prone to depressive episodes, so Ari had a predisposition to depression—though there were no signs of it yet. Ari's father felt at ease with the phone idea and even thought it would increase Ari's social contacts with texting and online interactions. He viewed the phone as an interactive tool and not one that isolated kids—despite the research that teens can become depressed when they only text and don't visit with friends.

Step Three: Understanding Your Child's Mind

After dinner, Ari had waited long enough and said again that he wanted to get a phone. He showed his folks all the research he'd done online and that the phone he'd picked out was top-of-the-line. His mother spoke to him quite directly: "Ari, what's up with your enthusiasm for a phone? Tell us what's on your mind. You seem really set on it."

Ari replied, "There isn't much to discuss. I want to text with the kids in the science club about projects we are working on. But mostly I want to download lots of apps to expand my interest in photography and video games. I also want to make videos to send my friends when I make science projects on my own. I think of the phone as a mini-computer more than a conversation device."

Ari's father responded, "You certainly have thought this through and seem to have made up your mind. I like your ideas."

Ari's mother reacted a bit differently: "I like your ideas about videoing your projects and sending them to your friends. It has an interactive feel to me. Is that what you had in mind?"

Ari: "Yeah, sort of. I know you are worried that I'll keep more to myself, but you shouldn't be so concerned. Everybody isn't like you, having tons of friends and social contacts. You're on your phone more than anyone I've ever seen, talking endlessly with your friends. Everybody doesn't use their phone that way. You have to catch up with my generation; the phone is a computer, just smaller and more accessible. I'll teach you how to use different applications to ease your mind. Chill. Don't worry so much."

For a ten-year-old, Ari was very mature and quite convincing. He seemed to empathize with his mother's doubts and knew her very well.

Step Four: Understanding Your Child's Development

Ari's mother took counsel with herself and realized she was blowing this whole thing out of proportion. Developmentally, Ari was on course as a preadolescent who was inventive, industrious, and even empathic. What more could she ask for? She relented.

Step Five: Problem Solving

Ari: "Well. I think we've discussed this long enough. Dad, you seem on board. What's the verdict between both of you? Enough talk. It's action time!" He let out a laugh as he said it.

Ari's mother and father spoke at once, to the surprise of both. "Go for it! Get online and pick out what you want."

Ari cheered and asked if he could use one of their credit cards, which they agreed to. He was overjoyed and looked forward to the phone being delivered in about two days. Using a landline, he called his science buddy and shared the news, which his mother got a kick out of. Ari was more social than she thought. She had overblown her fears.

The Parental Intelligence approach had succeeded valiantly. Ari and his folks collaborated and discussed their different points of view and all felt pleased with the decision. His parents realized further that Ari was probably going to be teaching them different ways to use a phone—ways that they didn't even know about. Roles were a bit reversed here: Ari was the expert and his parents were the learners. That pleased everyone!

CARRIE'S SIX-YEAR-OLD OBSESSION WITH VIDEO GAMES

Carrie was a rambunctious six-year-old in first grade with four older brothers, whom she was always trying to keep up with. Whenever they were in the car together, she watched a video on her oldest brother's iPad. Her brother was happy to share it with her and got a kick out of her shows. But she didn't talk with anyone as she watched, immersing herself completely in her movie choice of the day. She told this brother she wanted to keep his iPad for herself. She said that he "had enough techy things" and that she wanted her own. He told her that she could borrow it anytime, but he wasn't giving it up. "Why don't you ask Dad if he'll buy you one? He likes videos. He'll understand."

"He thinks I'm too young to have tech stuff," she said, annoyed.

"Don't give up so quickly," her brother said. "Asking can't hurt."

"Yes it can—if he says no!"

Carrie's mother was driving and overheard this conversation. She decided she would bring up the question with her husband that night.

Step One: Stepping Back

Carrie's mother knew that her daughter was prone to temper tantrums when she didn't get her way. She wanted to discuss "the iPad question" with her husband before they were confronted by their somewhat testy six-year-old—who was used to getting her way, as the baby in the family. She knew that asking for an iPad had been on Carrie's agenda for a few weeks now and wanted her husband's take on the matter.

Carrie's father felt Carrie was young to have an expensive tech device but knew there were a lot of opportunities for learning with an iPad, outside of just videos. She could draw, play educational games, and read on the iPad. He didn't want her isolating herself with videos all day, like an avid TV watcher, but they controlled how much TV Carrie watched, and she didn't protest their restrictions. He did say to his wife, "I want this to be a civil conversation—no temper tantrums. If she heads in that direction, we will abort the conversation until she settles down and is really open to an exploration of the device." Carrie's mother agreed.

Step Two: Self-Reflecting

Carrie's mother really had no reservations. In her mind, there was no difference between Carrie borrowing her brother's iPad and having her own to use and explore. She was calm about the whole thing. However, Carrie's father was a bit agitated about the money issue. He thought that she should have a sense of proportion about what things cost—even at age six. He was going to bring that up during the conversation: an iPad could cost $100, and it wasn't just a kid's toy.

Step Three: Understanding Your Child's Mind

Mother: "Carrie, I understand from your conversation with your brother in the car the other day that you want your own iPad. Can you tell us your thoughts about that?"

Carrie: "Yeah. I love my videos and I could watch them anytime without bothering anyone else."

Father: "Carrie, I don't want you watching videos all day long. That's just like you watching movies on TV, and it will keep you from doing a lot of other things. You are learning to read. How about spending time doing that, too?"

Carrie: "Daddy, you can read on an iPad. Don't you know that? I'll read on it. I promise. Please! This is such a good idea. You can even tell me how many videos I can watch each day and I'll listen. Really. Really. What do you think? I'll be so happy."

Father: "How about one video every other day, max? Then I want you to learn all the other kinds of things you can do on an iPad—like drawing, playing number games, learning new words to read, and other stuff. We can download different games to play together. What do you think of that?"

Carrie: "I think that's good. Yeah, really good. Will you play with me?"

Father: "Yes. We'll explore it together. But I want you to know that this is a big expense. Not a lot of six-year-olds get to have so much money spent on them for one thing. You must take really good care of it. What do you think about that?"

Carrie: "I'm sure I'll take good care of it, because I want it so much. I'll do all kinds of stuff with it if you teach me. I'll keep it in a special drawer in my desk when I'm not using it, so it will be safe. Is that what you mean?"

Father: (smiling) "Yes. That's what I mean. Okay, well Mommy and I will talk a little more about it and then let you know."

Carrie: "What? We aren't deciding right now? I want to get it NOW!"

Mother: "Carrie, you just yelled at us. You can be a little more patient while we think this through. Could you just wait ten minutes, please?"

Carrie: (Sensing a tantrum was a bad idea) "Okay. Sorry I yelled."

Step Four: Understanding Your Child's Development

Carrie's parents were already in agreement but did feel they were pushing the boundaries by buying such an expensive item for a six-year-old. They decided they would both spend time using it with her, showing her all the age-appropriate applications they could find. They were determined that the iPad would not become Carrie's video machine, for sure. It would be an educational tool. So, they agreed that an iPad fit Carrie's developmental age. And they also agreed that they would spend time with her using it, giving her the one-on-one time she craved.

Step Five: Problem Solving

Mother: "Okay, Carrie. We will all go shopping together to pick out an iPad. Daddy and I agreed. The rule is one video every other day, and both Daddy and I want to play on it with you so that we can all learn its different uses. I'm sure your brothers will help us, too. What do you think?"

Carrie: "I think you are really the nicest parents in the world. I love you. Can we go shopping after dinner tonight?"

Father: "I have a meeting tonight and want the three of us to do this together. Can you hold on and wait until Saturday, which is the day after tomorrow?"

Carrie: "Well, that sounds far away. But okay. Thanks, Mommy and Daddy."

Once again, Parental Intelligence was a successful route to solve a pretty easy question. Carrie's parents were pleased with Carrie's patience in waiting out the decision—and then waiting a few days to go shopping. This made them feel that their decision was developmentally on target. Carrie had the ability to tolerate waiting and that was important if she was going to use a sophisticated technological tool. They did believe she'd take good care of it and explore all of its advantages. Problem solved!

CHAPTER SEVEN

TEENS AND TECHNOLOGY: THE PARENTAL INTELLIGENCE WAY

*O*nline transgressions can be very complex, even in small communities. Here is an example of two seventh-grade girls faced with a cyberbullying incident that involved two sets of parents and the school. If not for the Parental Intelligence Way, this incident could have escalated into a uniquely hostile environment for all involved.

LIDIA REACTS TO CYBERBULLYING

Lidia is a thirteen-year-old eighth grader who loves going online. But when her friends set up an online profile on Instagram where people were asked to comment or vote for the prettiest girl among the four shown, she was worried to see her picture there. The ostensible idea of the kids who set this up was to show their friends pretty girls. However, one of the profile creators stuffed the virtual ballot box so that Lidia did not emerge victorious. The kids who set this up didn't realize that by creating the poll, the three remaining girls involved in the vote, including Lidia, would have their feelings hurt.

One of the kids who set up the profile, Evie, had a secret vengeance toward Lidia, whom she envied because Lidia was the class president. Evie deliberately wanted to distress Lidia, knowing her sensitivities to her body image. Evie had lost to Lidia in the recent election, and her *intention was to set up Lidia as a loser* by rigging the vote to show that Lidia was the least pretty. This ballot stuffing was done to cause harm to Lidia, making this intentional act one we could call cyberbullying. The voting was repeated for several days, making it a repetitive act.

Unfortunately, the post went viral around the school grade, though stayed in this one school and community, but Lidia was embarrassed and ashamed. She didn't want to return to school. She started having panic attacks, which had never happened before, and knew her anxiety was out of control. She didn't want to tell her parents at first, fearing they would take away her computer and phone access in order to protect her; when in actuality, taking her devices would make Lidia an even greater outlier from the other girls. Lidia's busy parents, however, had used the Parental Intelligence Way with Lidia since she was a young child, so she trusted them more than she feared their reactions and decided to confide in them. Lidia had found out that it was Evie who had initiated the incident and wanted her parents to know this truth—but she was worried because Lidia and Evie's parents were friendly, both having high-achieving daughters in the same grade and school. Both Lidia and Evie had a 99 percent average and excelled in many school leadership positions. Lidia had just beaten Evie in the class president election by a mere twenty votes, and they had vied in another club election, with Lidia winning there as well.

Evie was both frightened and excited when the post went viral, realizing she was harming Lidia more significantly than she had envisioned. She acted on impulse and anger; she was intentionally trying to get back at her competitor, wanting her to feel like a loser for once. Evie hadn't counted on the post going viral in their grade and feared the consequences when it got out that she was the cyberbully. She, too, wanted to let her parents know, so they could help her, but feared being punished severely for her unkind actions. She secretly didn't feel too guilty because she so hated Lidia's successes, but she knew instinctively to not reveal her lack of remorse; it would make her look really malicious, which in fact she was.

Two girls; two sets of very busy, professional parents who knew each other; a cyberbullying incident that swept the seventh grade in an upper-class neighborhood. This had escalated to quite a problem. Both girls wondered if the school would get involved, as the cyberbullying had evolved in the school arena. However, luckily for Evie, it at first appeared that she hadn't violated any civil rights that would require the school to legally intervene. The incident didn't quite qualify as sexual harassment, but it did border on student-on-student harassment, where the US Department of Education's Office of Civil Rights deemed that schools should take appropriate steps to contain the situation.

Once a school knows or reasonably should know of possible student-on-student harassment, it must take immediate and appropriate action to investigate or otherwise determine what occurred. If harassment has occurred, a school must take prompt and effective steps reasonably calculated to end the harassment, eliminate any hostile environment, and prevent its recurrence. These duties are a school's responsibility even if the misconduct also is covered by an anti-bullying policy and regardless of whether the student makes a complaint, asks the school to take action, or identifies the harassment as a form of discrimination (Hinduja and Patchin, 2015, *Bullying Beyond the Schoolyard*, 114; US Department of Education, 2010).

Both girls independently decided to tell their parents, and the viral nature of the incident was brought to the school principal's attention quickly by several unnamed students.

First, I will describe how the Parental Intelligence approach helped each family, and then I will explain how the parents and each girl spoke to the school principal to resolve the matter.

LIDIA AND HER PARENTS: THE PARENTAL INTELLIGENCE WAY

One early evening when she came home from work, Lidia's mother found her daughter hysterical in her room. She immediately called her husband and asked him to come home from work early, as she had never seen her daughter so distraught. He made it home in half an hour, and together they told Lidia that whatever was wrong, they would help her out. They knew instinctively that their knowledge of Parental Intelligence was going to help them sort this out—whatever it was—and that despite their busy schedules, Lidia's emotional well-being was going to take priority. The five steps of Parental Intelligence took place as follows:

Step One: Stepping Back

Lidia's parents knew to step back and not take any immediate actions as they contemplated their daughter's distraught condition. They knew to pause and stay calm, so Lidia could calm down. There was no precedent for this reaction of their daughter. They could see she was crying, breathing heavily, disoriented, and panicked.

Step Two: Self-Reflecting

Both parents were very worried, not having seen their child have a panic attack before. Lidia's mother, however, had experienced anxiety attacks herself and knew that whatever the reason, it could be contained. She was calmer than her husband, who felt irate that his daughter should be so distressed but followed his wife's lead in showing a calm front.

Step Three: Understanding Your Child's Mind

Mother: (Hugging Lidia, she spoke first.) "Lidia, sweetheart, what is the matter? You seem so distressed and even frightened. Do you want to share with us what's on your mind?"

Lidia: "I am scared and can't seem to control my breathing. Is this an anxiety attack? Oh, Mommy, I can't calm myself. I feel dizzy."

Mother: "Yes, dear. The way to help yourself first is to breathe slowly. Here, take your hands and cup them over your nose and mouth; breathe evenly and the feeling of dizziness will slowly subside. Don't worry about talking, just let yourself relax. We are here with you now. You aren't alone."

Lidia: "Gosh, that helps. I don't feel dizzy anymore, but I am really upset. Sorry, Daddy, you came home from work so early. I know how busy you both are. (Crying) Can I tell you something very private and awful that happened at school without you getting mad at anyone?"

Father: "Of course, we won't get mad at you or anyone for anything. Whatever it is we will work it out like we always do. Don't think for a second that we will blame or judge anyone—especially you. Do you feel up to telling us what happened?"

Lidia: "Yes. I want to. But it's hard to explain, since you don't know too much about Instagram. Remember Evie, your friend's daughter? She and some of our friends thought they'd play a kind of game on Instagram; they showed my picture with three other girls and had an online vote on who is prettiest. (Crying harder) I came in last. I was the loser! I'm so ugly. I hate myself."

Lidia's mother: "Angel, they were way out of line. First of all, you are pretty and shouldn't have to worry about your appearance, but I know you are sensitive to it. But who were the other girls, because this isn't making any sense to me."

Lidia told her mother the names of the other girls in the photo.

Lidia's mother: "All of those girls are pretty and nice friends of yours. Somebody did something to make you the loser. Can you think of any explanation?"

Lidia: "Well, it came out that Evie stuffed the virtual ballot box to make me the loser. You know how I beat her in the class president election and in the position for editor of the class yearbook? She didn't win either position, and I think she's been angry at me for a long time. She never speaks to me and is silent at all our meetings. But I wouldn't have thought she'd do such a mean thing to me. (Crying again) How could she?"

Father: "This rings of cyberbullying, sweetheart. Please don't think for a minute you are to blame, because you won fair and square in these elections. Evie is a very jealous little girl. Her parents, especially her mother, is very competitive and kind of a helicopter mother; she probably got her daughter really incensed about these elections. That's my immediate take on it. Don't worry about us being friends with Evie's parents. That's the least of this. It also has nothing to do with being pretty. Evie just came up with that because she knows you very well and that you've been worried about being attractive. As your dad, I know you shouldn't worry about that, but I do understand how hard it is to not worry about looks at your age."

Lidia: "Daddy, how do you know about cyberbullying? Why do you call it that?"

Father: "When someone intentionally uses the internet to hurt someone's feelings and cause them harm repeatedly, it is cyberbullying. She kept stuffing the ballot box, I believe, making it a repeated event and clearly was out to make you a loser. Sweetheart, people aren't as nice as you think sometimes. I hope she feels really guilty, or there's a real mental illness that we're dealing with here."

Mother: "Why do you say mental illness?"

Father: "Because it has a malicious intention to me. Evie wanted Lidia to be really upset. She's been harboring these angry feelings for a long time. The yearbook situation was three months ago, and the election was last week. Apparently, she—and I bet her mother—have been really up in arms over this. Lidia, I only explain this because I've seen cyberbullying before, and Evie probably had no idea it might get so big. Did it go viral in your grade?"

Lidia: "YES! To my amazement everyone started voting. I don't want to go back to school. I'm so humiliated and embarrassed to be the ugliest of all. Look at this picture. Don't I look awful?"

Father: "No. You don't look awful. You look like your pretty, wonderful self. There's no way you should feel like a loser. That's what Evie wanted. She finally wanted you to feel like a loser, because that's how she's feeling, I bet. She wanted to turn the tables on you. It was mean, sweetheart. It's hard for you to imagine meanness when you're so kind. That's one of the reasons you always win these elections, because you are smart, organized, efficient, and kind. People know you make a great leader."

Lidia: "Holy moly. This is overwhelming. I wonder if Evie told her parents. Oh, my gosh, I wonder if the school will get involved. Everybody knows about it. You should see all the text messages I have. I can't even read them all. Though it's nice that a lot of people are trying to make me feel better, and people are really talking against Evie."

Step Four: Understanding Your Child's Development

Lidia's mother was quiet for a while, contemplating that Lidia was going through puberty and that her body was changing rapidly. Lidia's period had come late, and she had developed her new svelte body shape just this year. Lidia's mother knew her daughter was uncomfortable with her body, though she was quite beautiful. They had just been bra shopping and Lidia had been embarrassed to see how much she had developed. The timing of all this couldn't have been worse, but maybe Evie intuited that. She was a troubled child with a troubled mother. They had to find a way to calm all this down.

Step Five: Problem Solving

Mother: "Lidia, what do you want us all to do to help you? There are many options. You had an anxiety attack because you felt alone and so unprepared for this incident and don't want it to persist any longer. What's on your mind about what we should all do? We're in this together."

Lidia: "Well, I don't actually feel as ugly now that we've talked about this. It was a crazy thing for Evie to do. I almost feel sorry for her. I wonder if she feels bad or is glad I suffered. I know we'll never be friends again and that it will mar your relationship with her parents. Sorry for that, but I know you don't blame me. And I really don't blame myself. You're right, Daddy. I won the elections fairly and never thought they were really that big a deal. It's because everyone worries so much about getting into colleges, even in eighth grade, that these things get blown out of whack. I do want to go back to school, and I'm sure the principal knows about it because everyone online is talking about it. I kind of think we should be proactive and one of you should call him. We should have a meeting, the three of us with him, to decide if we should do anything. I don't think I want to file a formal complaint about cyberbullying, Daddy—even though I know it's kind of a crime. I think the school should do whatever they do with things like this and that Evie should have to deal with what she did."

Father: "You are a very mature young lady, sweetheart. You really seem to be feeling a bit better. I'm so glad. Let's follow your plan and see what the principal says, and we'll consider his options. No formal complaint if you don't want it. I think that's smart. It would only make things get bigger, not smaller. We want it to really go away so that you can go back to school and lead your normal life."

Mother: "I agree to whatever you want Lidia. You're a brave girl to face the music by going back to school. People will see what a leader you really are and how self-confident you can be. If you get ridiculed, can you brush it off?"

Lidia: "I know I will feel hurt, but I don't want to panic over it again. For some reason I feel kind of settled. It's in Evie's court now, not mine. Actually, I feel like doing my homework and having dinner later. Does that sound okay?"

Mother and Father: (In unison) "Sounds good to me! You are amazing!"

So, at least in this family, the Parental Intelligence Way worked beautifully; it calmed everyone down quickly and helped them come to a reasonable resolution for the time being.

Let's take a look at Evie's family.

EVIE REACTS TO CYBERBULLYING

Evie took some counsel with herself and decided to act remorseful with her parents and tell them the whole story. She thought she could fake her feelings so that she didn't get in too much trouble. She didn't know what the principal would do, but he had already called her house and told her parents that they all had to meet with him the next morning. Due to that phone call, Evie didn't have to start the conversation; her parents confronted her openly. They were worried about what the principal had said, which was just that Evie did something to hurt another child's feelings and had to come to terms with it. Evie's parents were also believers in Parental Intelligence, so they had a clear head about how to approach whatever was going on.

Step One: Stepping Back

Evie's parents thought they should wait a bit before asking Evie why the principal had called, hoping she would initiate a conversation. They paused and waited.

Step Two: Self-Reflecting

Evie's mother was feeling kind of agitated, not used to having her daughter be in trouble. Her father was nervous, feeling that Evie had a mean streak in her and that maybe it came out some way. He was anxious and not willing to wait for Evie to come to them. So, her parents decided to tell her about the principal's call and see what she had to say.

Step Three: Understanding Your Child's Mind

Father: "Evie, the principal called and wants us to have a meeting—the three of us—with him tomorrow morning. What's this about? Do you know? He sounded upset, but he said it was better to explain in person than on the phone. He sounded cautious. What's up?"

Mother: "Before you start, remember we are with you in this, whatever it is, and will try to help you. But it's important to be honest about the trouble, which it sounds like it is."

Evie: "Well, it started out pretty innocently. I think Lidia's oversensitive. A few of us decided to do an Instagram thing where we took four pretty girls and made a contest about who was the prettiest. We had a virtual ballot, and everyone voted. To my surprise it went viral in the grade, and there were hundreds of votes, and Lidia came in last. That's about it."

Mother: "Why would Lidia come in last? She's very pretty. I know you don't like her, and she's beat you out in the recent elections, but she *is* pretty. What could have happened to make her last? She must have been really embarrassed. Personally, I don't like her too much myself. I think she's kind of full of herself, but that doesn't mean she isn't pretty. And she did win the elections fairly. I feel like there's more to all this, especially if the principal is involved."

Lidia: "Well, I'll tell the truth because it really doesn't matter. I kind of stuffed the ballot box so she'd come in last. She's been getting on my nerves with all these elections, and I don't think she cares about my feelings with losing the elections. So, I wanted her to know what it feels like to be a loser. That's exactly how I feel—that I'm a loser. That's all."

Father: "That's all? Evie, you did something mean. She won those elections fairly. I know you feel bad, but it wasn't her fault. You must have really felt terrible about losing. Sweetie, you feel like a loser? You are such an achiever, not a loser. These feelings seem to lie behind your actions—that weren't reasonable, to my way of thinking. I don't want to blame you for your feelings, and I won't, but why did you stuff the ballot box? What was that about making her a loser?"

Lidia: "She's always number one. I work very hard and have really good grades, and when we apply to Ivy League schools, she's going to put me in a tough position. I won't get in because we'll be chief competitors.

That's not fair, after all my hard work. I feel bad, I really do, that I hurt her, but she had it coming. I'm a loser and now she's one. She should know how it feels."

Mother: "I know how hard you try in school and that you're very successful. But when you say 'she had it coming,' what do you really mean to say? We aren't judging you, but we do want to help you. You sound really hostile, and that must feel pretty awful."

Lidia: "I don't like her. She always wins everything. Kids like her better than me. She thinks she's so special. *She* should know what it feels like to be humiliated once in a while."

Step Four: Understanding Your Child's Development

Evie's parents decided to step out of Evie's room for a few minutes and discuss what they were hearing. They liked Lidia's parents and knew she was a good, honest kid who never got in trouble. They were astounded by their daughter's coldness as she spoke of Lidia. Even though Evie's mother had been chagrined when Lidia won the elections, she hadn't thought of her daughter as being mean-spirited. She said to her husband, "I think we have a bigger problem here. The school might call this cyberbullying, because Evie did intend to make Lidia feel badly and kept the election going, so it has a repeated feeling to it. Lidia is trying to act like she's sorry, but she doesn't convince me at all. She can't hold back her animosity. Morally, she's developmentally off-course here. We need to get her some help. Her self-esteem is really low, if she feels like a loser in general. I agree with you. These feelings were behind her behavior. She's been feeling humiliated for months and we didn't know. I don't know if she's going to get suspended or what kind of punitive measure the principal will take. I hope Evie's parents didn't issue a complaint. Somehow, I don't think they would. They're really nice people, though I think we just lost a friendship. What's your take on all this?"

Father: "My understanding of cyberbullying is that it has to be intentional and malicious and repeated. I don't know if this qualifies, but if the school is involved already, it probably means it is at least on the border of a bullying incident—and that our daughter was the chief of the pack. I'm also worried about Evie's moral responsibility; her anger is out of control. I don't want to punish her, because she won't feel understood, only resentful. I'd like to suggest some professional help from a psychotherapist to help her work out her anger and faulty morality. What do you think? I also think we need some guidance, because somehow we've failed her in knowing when to take responsibility for a mistake."

Mother: "I like your way of thinking. Let's tell her your idea and see what she says."

Step Five: Problem Solving

Evie's parents go back in her room, where Evie is on the computer. She is chatting with friends online as if nothing unusual was going on.

Mother: "Evie, we are worried about you. What you did to Lidia was mean-spirited. I think you are internalizing the feeling of losing and I'd like you to get some help in thinking this through with a psychotherapist. Daddy agrees. What do you think?"

Evie: "A therapist? It was just a foolish mistake. I didn't know it would blow into something so big. I'm not an idiot or mental."

Father: "We're not calling you an idiot. We just feel you're confused about right and wrong, because you're feeling so angry at Lidia. I know you don't see your anger as a problem, but it is. It's hard to feel humiliated. I know what it's like to feel angry and out of control. I don't want you to suffer with that. Please consider a consultation with a therapist."

Evie: "Okay. It will probably make the principal go easier on me if he knows I'm willing to do that. I think everyone is blowing this out of proportion, but I'm willing to go for a meeting with a therapist. Some of my

friends see therapists, so it won't be so embarrassing—
or maybe they don't have to know."

Mother: "Therapy is a private matter. No one must
know. So, you'll go with us to the principal tomorrow
and we'll see what he has to say? Is that okay?"

Evie: "Sure. Are we done now? I have homework
to do."

Evie's parents were worried about Evie's response
but felt they were headed in the right direction. The
principal was pleased with the therapy plan and also
told Evie that if she posted an online apology to Lidia
for others to see then he would take no further action.
He did explain to Evie that her actions toward Lidia
were harassing and cyberbullying, which he couldn't
ever countenance again. Evie cried in embarrassment,
but she did what he said, and the incident blew over.
Evie did begin therapy and began to learn about how
the impact of her actions affected others.

THE PARENTAL INTELLIGENCE WAY

The Parental Intelligence Way helped both families
reach conclusions that were nonjudgmental, deeply
empathic, and helpful to their daughters. Eventually,
Evie's father called Lidia's father and apologized, admit-
ting his daughter had a lot to learn. He was remorseful,

even if his daughter hadn't reached that developmental step yet. The mothers were cordial when they saw each other now and then, but their friendships were over.

This incident was resolved rather smoothly without further harm done. In fact, both girls learned from it and took developmental strides from their experiences, in the long run. For being such busy parents, the two families managed a tough situation quite gracefully—and in a relatively short time. The structure of Parental Intelligence gave them the emotional organization they needed to weather the storm. The meaning behind both girls' feelings were understood with empathy and love.

The Parental Intelligence Way was a sound approach to solving these problems that had to do with technology choices. In each case, the parents of the children and teens collaborated to understand the meaning behind the presenting problems and to understand and empathize with their child or teen's wishes, intentions, and experiences. The five steps of Parental Intelligence helped the busy parents find a structured method to approach the situations that their children encountered. In a short amount of time, problems were resolved, and child-parent bonds were strengthened. Busy parents need to know a child-rearing approach that they can always depend on to meet their own and their children's needs in a short amount of time, reliably and empathically. Using Parental Intelligence is the way.

REFERENCES

Boyers, Lindsay (2018). Obesity in Children and Technology. Livestrong. http://www.livestrong.com /article/46320-obesity-children-technology.

Chan, Amanda (2011). 3 Ways Technology Affects Your Eyes. *LiveScience*. https://www.livescience .com/35579-3-ways-technology-affects-eyes.html.

Ebben, Paula (2012). How Technology Impacts Physical and Emotional Health. CBS Boston. https:// boston.cbslocal.com/2012/02/07/how-technology -impacts-physical-and-emotional-health/.

Ekman, Paul (2007). *Emotions Revealed: Recognizing Faces and Feelings to Improve Communication and Emotional Life.* Henry Holt, New York.

Hinduja, Sameer, and Patchin, Justin W. (2015). *Bullying Beyond the Schoolyard: Preventing and Responding to Cyberbullying.* Corwin, Sage Publication, Thousand Oaks, Calif.

Hollman, Laurie (2015). *Unlocking Parental Intelligence: Finding Meaning in Your Child's Behavior.* Familius, Sanger, Calif.

Hollman, Laurie (2020). *The Busy Parent's Guide to Managing Exhaustion in Children and Teens: The Parental Intelligence Way.* Familius, Sanger, Calif.

Tapscott, Don (1998). *Growing Up Digital: The Rise of the Net Generation.* McGraw Hill, New York.

Tapscott, Don (2009). *Grown Up Digital: How the Net Generation Is Changing Your World.* McGraw Hill, New York.

Twenge, Jean (2017). *iGen: Why Today's Super-Connected Kids Are Growing Up Less Rebellious, More Tolerant, Less Happy—and Completely Unprepared for Adulthood.* Atria Books, New York.

US Department of Education (2010). Dear Colleague Letter. US Department of Education Office for Civil Rights. https://www2.ed.gov/about/offices/list/ocr /letters/colleague-201010.html.

Zachos, Elaina (2015). Technology Is Changing the Millennial Brain. https://www.publicsource.org /technology-is-changing-the-millennial-brain/.

ABOUT THE AUTHOR

LAURIE HOLLMAN, PhD, is a psychoanalyst with specialized clinical training in infant-parent, child, adolescent, and adult psychotherapy. She specializes in modern parent-child relationships and is an award-winning author. She has been on the faculties of New York University and the Society for Psychoanalytic Training and Research, among others. She has written extensively on parenting for various publications, including the *Psychoanalytic Study of the Child*, *The International Journal of Infant Observation*, *The Inner World of the Mother*, *Newsday's Parents & Children Magazine*, and *Long Island Parent* in New York. She blogged for *Huffington Post* and currently blogs for *Thrive Global*. She also writes for *Active Family Magazine* in San Francisco and is a parenting expert for *Good Housekeeping* and *Bustle Lifestyle*. In addition, she is a contributor to the websites UpJourney and Mind Body Green. Her Mom's Choice Award winning books are: *Unlocking Parental Intelligence: Finding Meaning in Your Child's Behavior*; *The Busy Parent's Guide to Managing Anxiety in Children and Teens: The Parental Intelligence Way*; and *The Busy Parent's Guide to Managing Anger in Children and Teens: The Parental Intelligence Way*.

She has also recently written *The Busy Parent's Guide to Managing Exhaustion with Children and Teens* and *Are You Living with a Narcissist? How Narcissistic Men Impact Your Happiness, How to Identify Them, and How to Avoid Raising One*. Learn more on lauriehollmanphd.com.

She is married with two spirited adult sons.

ABOUT FAMILIUS

Visit Our Website: www.familius.com

Join Our Family

There are lots of ways to connect with us! Subscribe to our newsletters at www.familius.com to receive uplifting daily inspiration, essays from our Pater Familius, a free ebook every month, and the first word on special discounts and Familius news.

Get Bulk Discounts

If you feel a few friends and family might benefit from what you've read, let us know and we'll be happy to provide you with quantity discounts. Simply email us at orders@familius.com.

Connect

- Facebook: www.facebook.com/paterfamilius
- Twitter: @familiustalk, @paterfamilius1
- Pinterest: www.pinterest.com/familius
- Instagram: @familiustalk

The most important work you ever do will be within the walls of your own home.